ART Express

AUTHORS

Vesta A. H. Daniel

Lee Hanson

Kristen Pederson Marstaller

Susana R. Monteverde

Harcourt Brace & Company

Orlando   Atlanta   Austin   Boston   San Francisco   Chicago   Dallas   New York   Toronto   London

http://www.hbschool.com

Printed in the United States of America

ISBN 0-15-309317-X

4 5 6 7 8 9 10 048 2000 99

Dear Students,

Why do people create art? Do they do it to share their thoughts and feelings? To show the beauty of the world? To explore the human imagination? Whatever the reason, it must be a very powerful one, because people have been creating art since the beginning of human history. In fact, archaeologists are finding earlier and earlier works of art, created thousands of years ago.

The artworks you will discover in this book come to us from across the centuries and from around the world. They vary in age from the earliest cave paintings to the latest computer animations. They vary in form from a twisted piece of wire to a carved block of marble to a soaring cathedral.

In this book you will view the masterpieces of artists from many cultures. You will also develop your own skills and stretch your own imagination. As you try your hand at painting, sculpting, weaving, and other art forms, you, like all artists before you, will create art.

Sincerely,

The Authors

CONTENTS

UNIT 1 **Seeing Is Believing** • 14

 **UNIT 2** **Viewpoints.** 34

UNIT 4 # Harmony and Conflict. 74

LOOKING
AT ART

How do you make judgments about a work of art? Do you just say you like it or you don't?

To make a more meaningful judgment, take your time. For example, in a museum, don't try to see every artwork. Choose a few pieces, slow down, and really *look*.

1 **What do you see?** Think about the materials the artist used. Notice the main design elements, such as line, color, and shape. Take some time to describe the art.

2 **Ask yourself** how the artwork makes you feel. Does it remind you of anything? Think about how the art expresses thoughts and ideas.

3 **Focus on what is happening** in the art. What do you think the artist is trying to tell you?

4 **What do you think** of this work of art? Discuss your thoughts with others. You might also want to take notes in an art notebook.

KEEPING A
SKETCHBOOK

Many artists keep **sketchbooks**. They use their sketchbooks to make quick, simple drawings and to write notes about their artwork. Here is a sketch by Jerry Pinkney, an award-winning illustrator. You can see how the sketch led to the finished painting for the book *In for Winter, Out for Spring*.

The drawings and notes shown here are from a student's sketchbook.

My cat stretching

My family

Ideas for a
school mural:
— The history of our school

Here are some ways to use your sketchbook:

- Plan your artworks.
- Record ideas for future projects.
- Write your thoughts about other people's art.
- Show what you see around you as an artist.

AS YOU can see, both professional artists and student artists keep ongoing sketchbooks. You can, too. Choose a notebook that is large enough and flexible enough to draw in. (Unlined paper works best.) Decorate the cover. Then start sketching! Fill the pages with your ideas, notes, and drawings.

The Fall of the Cowboy, Frederic Remington
1895.

Seeing Is Believing

How does an

artist make a

viewer believe in

a scene?

Frederic Remington's Old West was a world of great natural beauty. It was also a world in which animals and people struggled daily to survive.

Look at *The Fall of the Cowboy*. What is made by nature in this scene, and what is made by people? Why might Remington have chosen to set this scene on a dark and cold day?

ABOUT FREDERIC REMINGTON

Frederic Remington's subject matter was the American West. Through his many illustrations, paintings, and sculptures, he created a permanent record of life on the frontier.

Images of Nature

How do you think these artists felt about the animals in the pictures?

Artists make images of the things that matter most to them. Sometimes they show animals that they depend on for survival.

Use your finger to trace the outlines of the bison in sculpture **A** and the deer on the jar **B**. Feel their flowing, rounded shapes. Natural objects often have this **organic** shape. Now look at the sharp angles of the designs at the top of the jar. This type of shape is called **geometric**.

What do you think the bison sculpture feels like? What about the jar? **Texture** is the word for the way a surface

Two Bison, unknown artist
Circa 12,000 B.C. Clay, each about 2 ft. long.
Cave at Le Tuc d'Audoubert, Ariège, France.

feels (A) or the way it appears to feel (B). An artist can use lines to show the texture of an object, even if it is painted on a smooth surface. Texture can make the object seem more lifelike or interesting.

 Water Jar with Deer, unknown artist of the Zuñi Native American people
Circa 1850. Clay, 10 3/4 in. high. Department of Anthropology, Smithsonian Institution, Washington, D.C.

IN THE STUDIO

MATERIALS

- **manila paper**
- **black paper**
- **glue**
- **colored pencils**
- **pastels (oil or chalk) or crayons**

Decorate a jar with a picture of an animal and geometric shapes. How can you use lines to show shape and texture?

1. On the manila paper, draw the outline of a pottery jar. Cut it out, and glue it to the black paper.

2. Draw an animal that matters to you. Think of what your animal would feel like if you touched it. Is it furry? Scaly? Feathery? Draw lines to show that texture.

3. Now decorate the rest of your pottery with geometric shapes.

Light and Shadow

How do artists make objects in drawings look rounded?

A Spray of a Plant, **Leonardo da Vinci**
The Royal Collection, Windsor Castle, England.

Paper is flat, or **two-dimensional**. But most of the objects artists draw are not flat. They have rounded **three-dimensional form** rather than flat shape. Look at how the artist showed the roundness of the fruit in picture **A**. He used tiny lines, or **hatching**. These lines also create shadows on the leaves and around the plant.

B

The Lighthouse at Two Lights,
Edward Hopper
1929. Oil on canvas, 29 1/2 X 43 1/2 in.
Metropolitan Museum of Art, New York.

18

Can you tell where the sun is in picture **B**? You can if you notice the **highlighting** along the right side of the tower and on the walls. Look at how the artist made some of the walls darker. The lightness or darkness of a color is its **value**. You can add a little black to any color to give it a darker value.

Can you find the shadows in picture **C**? How did the artist show the form of the sneakers?

C Student artwork

IN THE STUDIO

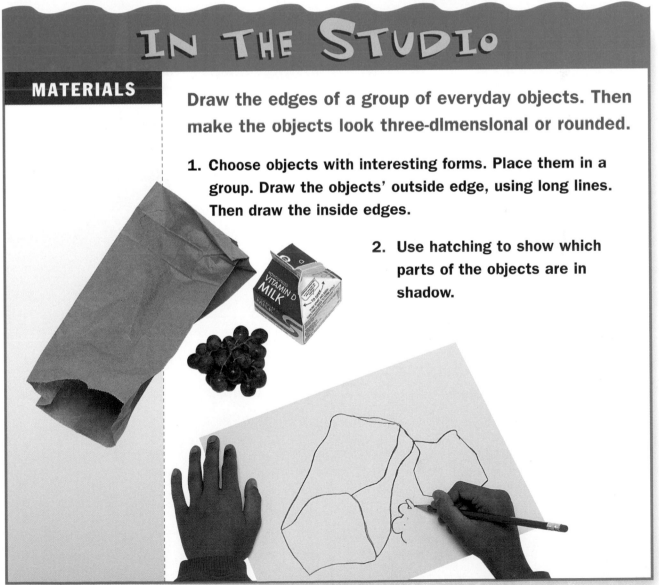

MATERIALS

Draw the edges of a group of everyday objects. Then make the objects look three-dimensional or rounded.

1. Choose objects with interesting forms. Place them in a group. Draw the objects' outside edge, using long lines. Then draw the inside edges.

2. Use hatching to show which parts of the objects are in shadow.

The Natural Art of Barbara Bash

Nature illustrators use both their artistic talent and their scientific knowledge. They create images of nature that seem to come to life.

▲ Barbara Bash

Long ago, most nature illustrators were also scientists. Before the camera was invented, these scientists roamed the world, looking for new plants and animals. They drew what they saw, clearly and carefully. These drawings were the only way other people could see many natural wonders. Today, of course, we have other ways to view nature. Still, nature illustrators like Barbara Bash can help us understand the world we live in.

Barbara Bash is both an author and an illustrator. She creates books that combine information about nature with a love of creatures and plants. Before she set about writing and illustrating *Tree of Life: The World of the African Baobab,* she did careful research. She wanted her drawings to be accurate. She also wanted to share her love of nature.

Look at the illustration of bushbabies on this page. How did Barbara Bash use color, texture, and line to bring these animals to life? What do you think a bushbaby would feel like if you could pet it?

◀ *Tree of Life: The World of the African Baobab,* by Barbara Bash

WHAT DO YOU THINK ?

▶ **What does this art communicate about the animals and their environment?**

▶ **What techniques did Barbara Bash use to make the bushbabies look soft?**

The Illusion of Distance

How do artists make some things look close and others look far away?

Put your finger on the part of the scene in picture **A** that looks farthest away. This is the **background** of the painting. Now point to the **foreground**, the part of the painting that looks closest to you. Where do you think the **middle ground** is in picture A? Can you point to the foreground, middle ground, and background in picture **B**?

In real life, moisture in the air makes things that are far away look pale and dull. That is why artists often use pale or dull colors to paint backgrounds. In this way, they show **atmospheric perspective**.

 View from Mount Holyoke, Northampton, Massachusetts, after a Thunderstorm–The Oxbow, **Thomas Cole**
1836. Oil on canvas, 51 1/2 X 76 in.
Metropolitan Museum of Art, New York.

Look at how the hill in the foreground of picture A **overlaps** the river valley. When two objects in a picture overlap, the object that is blocked out is the one that is farther away. Can you find an example of overlapping in picture B?

 Gould's Inlet, Anna Belle Lee Washington
1993. Oil on canvas, 18 X 24 in.

IN THE STUDIO

MATERIALS

- wax paper
- construction paper or other colored paper
- white paper
- scissors
- glue
- stapler

Create a country or city scene. Use overlapping to show background and foreground.

1. Think of a scene in which some things are far away and some are closer. Choose two colors of paper. Cut out background objects and foreground objects from different colors.

2. Glue down the background objects first. Over that, place a sheet of wax paper. Next, glue down your foreground objects. Staple a paper frame around the edges of your artwork.

Into the Scene

How do artists "pull" viewers into their paintings?

Where does the road in this painting end? How can you tell? Put your finger on the part of the road that looks farthest away. You have just found the **vanishing point**. Notice how the sides of the road come closer together until they meet at the vanishing point.

Avenue of the Alyscamps,
Vincent van Gogh
1888. Oil on canvas, 36 1/4 in. X 29 1/8 in.
Collection of Mrs. A. Mettler-Weber,
Zollikon, Switzerland.

When artists paint scenes this way, they are using **linear perspective**. Look at the top half of the picture. The tops of the trees form another pair of lines that come together at the vanishing point. What would happen if you could walk to this point?

Linear perspective is one way that artists show depth. Sometimes it can make you feel as if you could walk right *into* the scene.

IN THE STUDIO

MATERIALS

- ruler
- soft pencils
- drawing paper

Use linear perspective to draw a scene that pulls the viewer into it.

1. Think of a scene that includes pairs of lines, such as a road or railroad tracks.

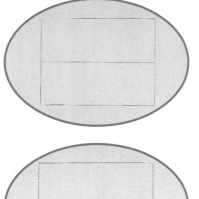

2. Draw a picture frame. Use your ruler to draw a horizontal line representing the farthest point you can see. This is the horizon line. In the middle of that line, mark a vanishing point.

3. Now draw the lines for your road or railroad tracks. Line up your ruler with the horizon line so that your lines come together at the vanishing point. Then add objects, details, and color to the scene.

Set Designer

How do you make a 400-year-old play fun for today? How do you turn a house inside out in five seconds? How do you fit Elmo and Ruthie into Big Bird's nest with him for a sleep-over? For answers to these questions, you need to talk to **Bob Phillips.** *As a set designer, Bob Phillips creates scenery for stage, television, and movies. Here he shares some of his designs and talks about his career.*

▼ **Design for** *Two Gentlemen of Verona* **at the Orlando Shakespeare Festival**

"In my full-time job, I'm the art director for *Sesame Street.* In my spare time, I get to travel all over the United States to design scenery for regional theaters. For *Two Gentlemen of Verona*, the director moved up the time of Shakespeare's play from the 1500s to 1959 and added rock-and-roll music and radio deejays. I designed the signs on the poles to rotate to show different messages in different scenes.

▲ Design for Molière's *The School for Wives* at the Pennsylvania Shakespeare Festival

"In *The School for Wives*, two of the actors were also scene changers. They spun the walls around. Motors backstage rotated the ceiling and the benches, and the chandeliers flew in on wires. We were able to change the scene from outside to inside in less than five seconds.

"For *Sesame Street*'s twenty-fifth anniversary, we doubled the size of the set. The production designer and I used hundreds of photos of New York streets and buildings to create the design. That was a great project.

"Every day we make special things to help the puppeteers in their work. I love this job. I was thrilled when I found out that set design was actually a career. I can't imagine myself doing anything different."

▲ Bob Phillips on *Sesame Street* set

WHAT
DO
YOU
THINK
?

▶ What kinds of skills would be helpful to a set designer?

▶ What information do you think the director of a play would give to the set designer?

27

Impressions of Light

How did one group of artists try to capture special moments?

Summertime, **Mary Cassatt**
1894. Oil on canvas, 28 7/8 in. X 39 3/8 in.
Armand Hammer Museum of Art and
Cultural Center, Los Angeles.

What season or time of day is shown in each of these paintings? How can you tell? The artists who painted pictures **A** and **B** tried to capture a quick, fleeting look, or impression. These painters were part of a group called the **Impressionists**. Impressionism started in France in the 1870s. Notice how the light hits the water in pictures A and B. With your finger, brush over each stroke in A as if you

Harp of the Winds: A View on the Seine,
Homer Dodge Martin
1895. Oil on canvas, 28 3/4 in. X 40 3/4 in.
Metropolitan Museum of Art, New York.

were painting it yourself. These **brushstrokes** show the movement of the water.

Can you find where the top part of picture B is almost exactly like the bottom part? This is called **horizontal symmetry**. In this painting the water is like a mirror, reflecting everything above it.

 Student artwork

IN THE STUDIO

MATERIALS

- large sheets of tagboard or other white paper
- watercolors
- tempera paints
- paintbrushes

Make a painting that shows a reflection in water.

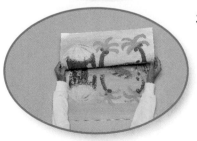

1. Fold a piece of paper the long way, and then open it.

2. Using the watercolors, paint two backgrounds—a sky background above the fold, and a lake background below the fold. Let dry. Using the tempera paints, add objects above the fold, such as plants, trees, and buildings. These are the objects on the water's bank.

3. After completing each object, fold the paper so that the tempera paint prints on the bottom half. This is the reflection in the lake.

Showing Movement

How do artists make objects seem to be moving?

Some artists create two-dimensional artwork such as paintings and drawings. Other artists create three-dimensional works of art called **sculptures**. Sculptures can be almost comically simple, such as **A**, or detailed and dramatic, such as **B**.

Sculptors often use long, slanting lines to make an object look as if it is moving. Find some slanting, or **diagonal**, lines in sculptures A and B. Which part of each sculpture seems to be moving? With your finger, trace some long, diagonal lines in sculpture B. Does this sculpture show a lot of movement or a little movement? Why do you think so?

Imagine that sculpture B could come to life. What might happen next?

Horse and Rider, Alexander Calder
Circa 1950. Wire, 14 in. X 17 in. X 5 1/2 in.
Galerie Maeght, Paris.

IN THE STUDIO

MATERIALS

- wire or pipe cleaner

Make a wire sculpture of an animal. How can you show movement?

1. Use three pieces of wire for your basic "skeleton."

2. Twist the wires around each other to create an animal.

3. Bend parts of your animal to show a movement such as running or leaping.

Artists use illusions to create images of their environments.

In this unit, you have learned about some of the ways artists show movement, texture, and distance. These techniques can make a work of art come to life. Look at this sculpture in Dallas, Texas. The artist is showing an important part of Texas heritage in an unusual way. This life-size cattle drive is placed in the middle of a large, bustling city!

Pioneer Plaza, **Robert Summers**
Under construction. Dallas, TX.

What Did I Learn?

- **HOW** did this artist make the cattle seem to move? How would this sculpture be different if the cattle seemed to be standing still?

- **FIND** an artwork in this unit that is like this sculpture in some way. How are the two pieces alike? How are they different?

- **THINK** about the art you created in this unit. How did you show movement? How did you show texture and distance? What other techniques did you use?

- **FIND** an example of an artwork in this unit that shows distance. Explain what techniques the artist used.

Roosevelt dime,
based on Burke's plaque.

Franklin Delano Roosevelt, Selma Burke
Bronze, 3 ft. 6 in. X 2 ft. 6 in.

Viewpoints

How can art

express how

people feel about

a country and

its history?

Throughout the history of the United States, artists have shown their patriotism through art. They have made pictures and sculptures that tell about important American heroes, ideas, and events.

This plaque was made by artist Selma Burke to honor President Franklin Delano Roosevelt. Burke said she wanted this to be the best piece of sculpture she had ever done? Why do you think she felt this way?

ABOUT SELMA BURKE

Dr. Selma Burke studied art at Sarah Lawrence College and Columbia University. She was in the Navy during World War II when she created her sculpture of the president.

Portraits

What can you tell about these two people from their pictures?

A **portrait** is a picture of a person. Portraits are often created to tell about an important person's life and work. Why do you think the artist decided to show President George Washington in this **pose**, or position? The sword and the pen in portrait **A** are **symbols** of Washington's special skills and talents. What special skill do you think each symbol stands for?

Mary McLeod Bethune started a women's college in Florida. On which parts of her portrait **B** did the painter put the most **emphasis**, or importance? What kind of person do you think Bethune was, judging from her portrait?

A *George Washington*, Gilbert Stuart

B *Mary McLeod Bethune*, Betsy Graves Reyneau
1943–44. Oil on canvas. National Portrait Gallery, Washington, D.C.

When you draw a portrait, look carefully at the person's face. Do not try to draw from memory. Notice the **proportions** of the face. Proportion is the size and placement of the features when you compare them with each other. Where are the eyes compared with the ears? How big is the forehead compared with the whole head? A grid like the one shown here can help you draw portraits.

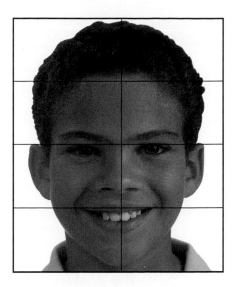

IN THE STUDIO

MATERIALS

- model
- white paper for background, neck, and shoulders
- smaller white paper for face
- soft pencil
- ruler
- watercolors
- paintbrushes
- pastels (oil or chalk) or crayons
- scissors
- glue

Draw a portrait of a person. Show the person's head and shoulders. Use natural-looking proportions.

1. First, choose a model (a person to pose for you). Then use watercolors to paint a background on the large sheet. Choose colors that express a feeling or an attitude about the person.

2. Use a ruler and a pencil to draw a light grid. Draw the person's face in the grid. Then use pastels or crayons to redraw your lines, adding color and details.

3. Cut out the face, and glue it to the background, leaving room for the neck and shoulders. Remember to look at your model carefully. Use pastels or crayons to draw in the neck and shoulders.

Colors and Feelings

How do you think the artists felt about these scenes of the past?

American flags! Balloons! A band marching down Main Street! How would you feel if you were standing on the curb watching the parade in picture **A**? Artists can use bright colors to create a **mood**, or feeling, of excitement. They can use the colors of the American flag to make Americans feel proud.

 A Really Swell Parade Down Main Street, Jane Wooster Scott

What do you think it would feel like to be a student in picture **B**, *The Country School*? Why? What colors did the artist use to create this mood? **Warm colors** (reds, oranges, yellows) can make us feel warm and happy. **Cool colors**, such as blues and violets, can make us feel cool. How else did the artist show his feelings about this old-fashioned school?

The Country School, **Winslow Homer**
1871. Oil on canvas, 21 3/8 X 38 3/8 in.
The Saint Louis Art Museum, St. Louis, MO.

IN THE STUDIO

MATERIALS

- **watercolor paper**
- **watercolors**
- **paintbrushes**

Paint with the colors of the past.

Imagine you are living far in the future. Paint a picture that makes some part of life today seem like "the good old days." Use warm colors to make viewers feel good about what is happening in your scene.

Magazine Art

Children's magazines have been popular in the United States since 1829.

Nineteenth-century children did not have TVs or videos, but they did have wonderful books and magazines. In fact, many of the books they read, such as *Alice in Wonderland* and *The Adventures of Tom Sawyer,* are still popular with young readers today.

The most popular children's publication back then was called *St. Nicholas Magazine.* Look at this cover and these illustrations. If you didn't look at the date, how could you tell that this art was done long ago?

▶ **Cover of St. Nicholas Magazine, July 1926**

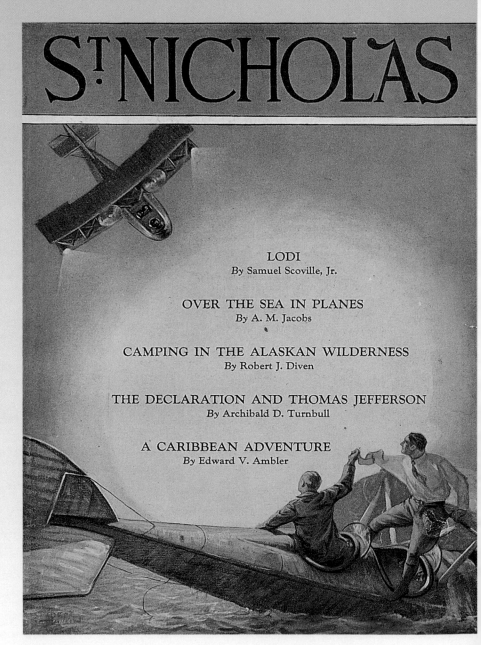

St NICHOLAS

LODI
By Samuel Scoville, Jr.

OVER THE SEA IN PLANES
By A. M. Jacobs

CAMPING IN THE ALASKAN WILDERNESS
By Robert J. Diven

THE DECLARATION AND THOMAS JEFFERSON
By Archibald D. Turnbull

A CARIBBEAN ADVENTURE
By Edward V. Ambler

"Great Grandmother's Girlhood"

"The Mistletoe Hung in the Castle Hall..."

WHAT DO **YOU** THINK ?

How would you describe the colors in these illustrations?

Do you think a publisher would use this type of art today? Explain.

Mosaics

How do artists turn walls into special places of honor?

Mosaics are pictures made with many small pieces called **tesserae** [TEH•suh•ree]. Mosaic **A** tells the story of the beginning of a city. It was created in an **abstract** style. The people in A do not look like people do in the natural world. What feeling might the artist want viewers to have about this new city? How do you know?

Mosaic **B** was made to decorate a Roman tomb. It was created in a **nonrepresentational** style. The shapes and colors in B do not look like objects you recognize. Why might this wall honor the dead more than a plain wall?

 Detail from a mural in Shalom Mayer Tower, Nachum Gutman
1965–66. Tile, about 15 ft. 8 in. X 55 ft. 8 in. (entire mural). Tel Aviv, Israel.

 Detail from the *Greca* Mausoleum of Galla Placidia
A.D. 424–450. Tile, width about 2 ft.
Ravenna, Italy.

IN THE STUDIO

MATERIALS

- colored stones
- beads
- cut paper
- glue
- large sheet of heavy cardboard

Work with a group to make a mosaic.

First, plan your mosaic together. Decide if you want to tell a story or make an abstract design. Then sketch your plan in pencil on a sheet of heavy cardboard. Glue colored stones, beads, and cut paper to the cardboard to make your mosaic.

Images That Inspire

How do these works of art make you feel about the United States?

These three works of art honor American values. They show ideas that are traditionally important to Americans. Find the torch in picture **A**. What do you think this symbol stands for? In picture **B**, the suitcases might be symbols of moving. The people in this picture are trying to move to a better place. What symbol can you find in picture **C**? What values do you think this scene represents?

Find some diagonal lines in pictures B and C. How do these repeated diagonal lines help you understand the people's struggle?

 Liberty Enlightening the World, **Frédéric-Auguste Bartholdi**
1886. Copper, 151 ft. 1 in. tall (toe to torch).
New York Harbor, New York.

 Panel 40 from *The Migration Series,* **Jacob Lawrence**
1940–41. Tempera and gesso on composition board, 18 in. X 12 in.
Museum of Modern Art, New York.

Scale is the size of an object in an artwork compared to its real size. Many public **statues** have a powerful effect on people because they have such a grand scale—they are much larger than life. How large is the Statue of Liberty? About fifteen fifth graders can stand inside its crown!

 The Marine Corps Memorial, Felix W. de Weldon
Bronze. Arlington, VA.

IN THE STUDIO

MATERIALS

- old magazines
- scissors
- poster board
- glue

Create a photomontage, a group of photos that form one picture. Express an American value.

1. **Think about values such as freedom, courage, and equality. Choose one that you would like to express. Find and cut out magazine photos that show this value.**

2. **Arrange your photos on the poster board. Use overlapping. Try to give emphasis to photos that make a strong statement. Glue the pictures down. Give your photomontage a title.**

HEROIC STATUES

Communities across America honor their heroes with statues.

One of the greatest honors a community can give someone is to put up a statue. Look at the statues on these pages. The people of Phoenix, Arizona, honored the Navajo Code Talkers—talented men from that area who served bravely in World War II. The people of Richmond, Virginia, honored Arthur Ashe—a local boy who grew up to be an international tennis star. Among the statues of heroes in our nation's capital is one that honors all the women who served the United States in the Vietnam War. What decisions did each sculptor have to make in order to create these statues?

▲ Navajo Code Talker

▲ Vietnam Women's Memorial

▲ Arthur Ashe

WHAT
DO
YOU
THINK
?

▷ What qualities do the three statues have in common?

▷ Look at the setting, or background, of each statue. How does it contribute to the effect?

The Power of the Poster

What were these posters designed to do?

Most posters are meant to attract people's attention. They use bright colors, bold words, and simple, powerful pictures. What did the artist do with poster **A** to attract your attention?

Look at Uncle Sam's finger. It's been **foreshortened**, or made shorter, to appear to be pointing *right at you*. Now look at the **type**, or printing. How does it get your attention? This poster is persuasive. The artist wanted people to join the army. He wanted them to feel a personal duty to their country.

How does poster **B** make you keep looking at it? Now look at poster **C**. How did the artist create suspense? How does this poster make you feel about the Olympic Games?

A *Uncle Sam Wants You,* James Montgomery Flagg

48

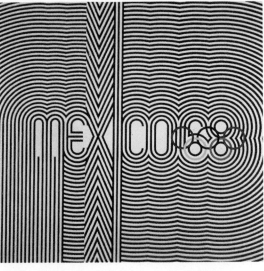

Mexico City Olympic Games, Lance Wyman
1968.

 B

Tokyo Olympic Games, Yusaku Kamekura
1964.

C

IN THE STUDIO

MATERIALS

- brightly colored paper
- poster paints
- paintbrushes
- markers
- poster board
- glue
- scissors

Design a poster that persuades viewers to feel or to do something.

1. Decide on the purpose of your poster.

2. Sketch a poster design. View your sketch from a distance. Are your pictures simple and powerful? Are your words exciting and easy to read?

3. Complete your poster, using colored paper, paints, and markers.

49

Pop Art

What does this can of peaches mean to you?

Can a painting of a can of peaches be a work of art? What about six rubber balls? In the world of **Pop Art**, the answer is yes. *Pop* is short for *popular*. Pop Art often shows things that are popular, such as the canned food in picure **A**. Pop artists have a message: Anything in our culture can become art, if an artist sees it that way. Do you agree? Why or why not?

Notice the thick, textured paint in picture **B**. This technique is called **impasto** painting. How does the paint in picture B look different from the paint in picture A? Which colors and shapes are repeated in B? Repeated objects and elements give a painting **unity**. They make it come together as a whole. What differences can you find among the balls? Differences, or **variety**, can make a painting more interesting.

A

***Peach Halves,* Andy Warhol**
1960. Synthetic polymer paint on canvas,
70 in. X 54 in.

Untitled, **Wayne Thiebaud**
1967. Oil on canvas, 12 1/4 in. X 14 1/4 in.
Private collection.

IN THE STUDIO

MATERIALS

- **tempera paints**
- **paintbrushes**
- **dry wheat paste**
- **cardboard**
- **craft sticks**
- **newsprint**

Make an impasto painting of a common object. Show the object's color and texture.

1. **Paint the back of your cardboard. Attach a piece of newsprint to the wet paint. This will help keep the cardboard from bending when you paint the front of it.**

2. **Choose an object you look at every day. (This should be a human-made object.)**

3. **Mix wheat paste with your paint. Paint a picture of your object, using the side of a craft stick.**

51

Art can convey attitudes about people, places, and events.

Think about some of the artwork you saw in this unit. How did the artists show they were proud of their country? The artwork on this page shows a great deal of pride, too. This "living flag" is made of 10,000 sailors. The artist, Arthur Mole, created patriotic photographs like this in many parts of the country.

The Living American Flag, Arthur Mole
Circa World War I. 10,000 men. U.S. Naval Training Station, Great Lakes, IL.

What Did I Learn?

- **THINK** about the artwork you created in this unit. What feelings did you express about people and places?

- **LOOK** back through the unit. Find examples of symbols in the art. What do these symbols stand for? Why do you think the artists chose these symbols?

- **FIND** two artworks in this unit that you especially like. Tell what you think the artists' viewpoints are. How did they show those viewpoints?

- **NAME** an artwork that tells about a time in American history. How does the artist help you understand more about that time?

Clothed Automobile, Salvador Dalí
1941. Oil on cardboard, 15 1/2 in. X 10 1/2 in.
Fundación Gala–Salvador Dalí, Figueras, Spain.

Unexpected Art

How can art

be funny or

surprising?

Every artist must have an active imagination. Some artists also have a good sense of humor. What is amusing about this painting? How is it different from what you might expect?

Salvador Dalí (SAHL•vuh•dawr dah•LEE) is one of many painters whose works often surprise us. He liked to show ordinary objects in unexpected ways. Sometimes he combined two or more ordinary things to create something extraordinary.

As you look at and create art in this unit, keep your eyes open for surprises. You might even surprise yourself!

ABOUT SALVADOR DALÍ

Salvador Dalí was born in Spain but moved to the United States during World War II. He is known for his strange, dreamlike images.

Experimenting with Space

How can simple shapes create big surprises?

Look at the black shape in picture **A**. Now look at the white shapes. Do you see two different pictures? If you could make up two different titles for A, what would they be? **Positive space** describes the shapes, lines, and forms in a work of art. **Negative space** describes the empty space around them. Picture A is playing with positive and negative space. You see something different depending on which space you look at.

A Vase or faces?

B

The Swimmer in the Aquarium, **Henri Matisse**
Circa 1944. Gouache on paper cutouts, 16 5/8 in. X 25 5/8 in.
Museum of Modern Art, New York.

Picture **B** is a **collage**. It was made by pasting pieces of cut paper together. The background of this picture is made of bright colors. The shape of the swimmer is simply white. Usually, the shapes and objects in a picture are filled with color, and the background is empty. What part of this collage is empty? What part is the negative space? It's hard to say!

IN THE STUDIO

MATERIALS

- **white paper**
- **dark paper**
- **scissors**
- **glue**

Make a white cutout against a dark background. Make both the positive and the negative space interesting.

1. **Fold a sheet of white paper the long way. Draw one half of a design on your folded paper. Get fancy! Think about what shapes and spaces you want the viewer to see.**

2. **Cut out your design, and unfold the paper.**

3. **Glue your white paper against a piece of dark paper. How is the design different when you look at the space in different ways?**

The Art of Illusion

How can colors and shapes trick your eyes?

A Optical illusion

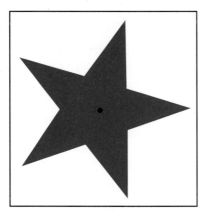

Stare at the center of the red star picture in **A** while you count to thirty. Then look at the black dot in the white space. What do you see? Are you sure? If it's not really there, it is an **optical illusion**. What do you see when you stare at picture **B**? At picture **C**? Art that plays tricks on your eyes is called **Op Art**. Op (short for *optical*) Art is meant to dazzle your eyes and fool your brain.

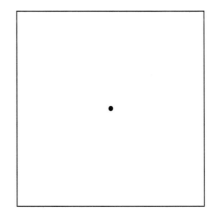

Suspension, **Bridget Riley**
1964. Emulsion on wood, 45 3/4 in. X 45 7/8 in.
Walker Art Center, Minneapolis, MN.

58

Colors that are across from each other on the color wheel are called **complementary colors**. These colors seem to move and change when they are next to each other, as you can see in picture C. How else does this painting fool your eyes?

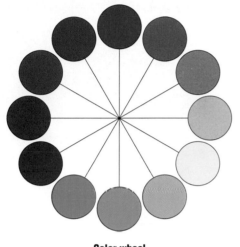

Color wheel

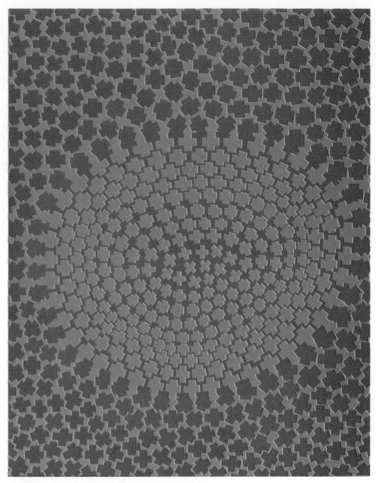

 Plus Reversed, Richard Anuszkiewicz
1960. Oil on canvas, 74 5/8 in. X 58 1/4 in.
Archer M. Huntington Art Gallery, The University
of Texas at Austin.

IN THE STUDIO

MATERIALS

- poster board
- brightly colored construction paper
- scissors
- glue

Make a cut-paper collage.

Cut shapes out of paper, and glue them onto a background. Use complementary colors. Can you make the shapes seem to move?

Can You Believe Your Eyes?

Some works of art make you stop and stare.

Over two hundred years ago, an American artist named Charles Willson Peale decided to fool visitors to his home. Peale painted a life-size staircase on one wall. Then he framed the painting with a real step and a real doorway. Peale fooled many, many visitors, including George Washington.

Artists today still enjoy fooling their viewers. Look at the outdoor scene painted on a building in Fort Worth, Texas. How does it fool the eye?

◄ *The Staircase Group,* Charles Willson Peale 1795. Philadelphia Museum of Art: The George W. Elkins Collection

▲ Chisholm Trail facade, Jet Building
Fort Worth, Texas

WHAT
DO
YOU
THINK
?

▶ How does the setting of each painting help the artist fool the viewer?

▶ Do you think people enjoy being fooled this way? Why or why not?

61

Imaginary Worlds

How can an artist

tell a fantasy story?

***Rumble and Mist*, James Gurney**
1995.

This painting shows a scene from James Gurney's book *Dinotopia: The World Beneath.* Illustrators can create make-believe worlds, filled with fantastic scenes. Which things in this painting might exist in the real world? Which parts tell us that the scene is imaginary?

Look at the water in this scene. Find some places where the artist used highlighting to show where sunlight hits the water. Find some warm colors in the painting. What kind of mood do these colors help create?

Where do you think the flying creatures with riders might be going? What do you think might happen when they get there? What else can you learn about this story from the art?

IN THE STUDIO

MATERIALS

- cardboard box (shoe box or larger)
- colored paper
- colored markers
- scissors
- modeling clay
- string
- tape

Work alone or in a group. Create a diorama of an imaginary world.

1. Use markers or colored paper to create a background on the back wall of your box.

2. Use modeling clay to create characters, buildings, and other things to place inside your diorama.

3. You may want to use string and tape to hang flying creatures or objects from the ceiling of your diorama.

Assembled Art

How can an artist use unusual objects to create art?

An **assemblage** is a group of objects that are put together, or assembled. Where would you look for objects to create an assemblage like **A** or **B**? Where do you think these artists found these objects?

We often use the word *junk* to describe things that are unwanted. But artists can use unwanted objects to create some exciting surprises. John Outterbridge combined unwanted metals and fabric into an assembled sculpture. This assemblage expresses ideas about cars and about California.

Louise Nevelson made her wall-sized sculpture from furniture pieces and other wooden items. After she assembled the pieces, she painted them all gold to give the assemblage unity. How else does the assemblage show unity?

A

California Crosswalk,
John Outterbridge
1979. Metals, wire, cloth, other mixed media, 3 ft. 6 in. X 3 ft. California Afro-American Museum Foundation, Los Angeles.

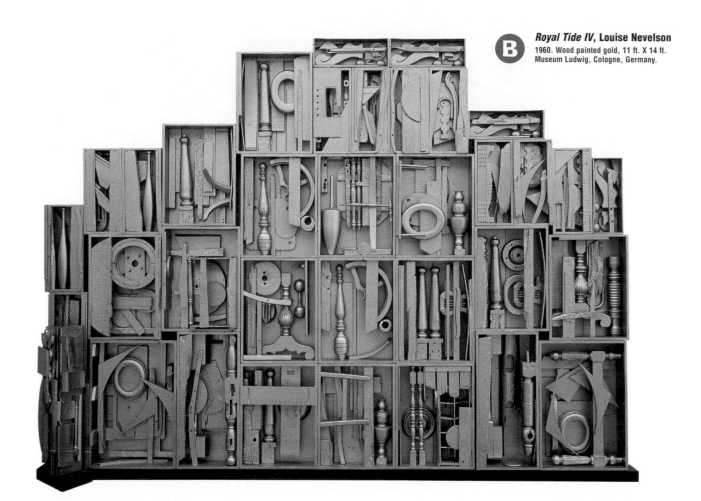

IN THE STUDIO

MATERIALS

- unwanted objects
- strong glue
- large sheets of cardboard or foamcore

Create an assemblage.

Collect objects of different shapes and sizes. (First check to be sure nobody wants these items.) Experiment with your objects. Find interesting ways to fit them together to express unity and variety. Glue your objects to the cardboard or foamcore in the arrangement you like best.

The Power of Art

Art can bring beauty to a neighborhood. It can also bring people together.

Lily Yeh is an artist who cares about communities. Many young artists show they also care by working with her.

This neighborhood is in Philadelphia. It was once very run-down, and many people who lived there wished they could move. Lily Yeh helped them change all that. Many people in the neighborhood, including young people, worked together. First they built an "art park." Later, they went on to the other projects shown here. What messages do these projects send about this community?

◀ **Lily Yeh working on the *Tree of Life* mural**

Meditation Park

▶ **Why do you think Lily Yeh chose the title**
***Tree of Life* for this mural?**

▶ **Do you think this community art will still be**
valuable to future generations? Explain.

Double Takes

What is strange about each of these paintings?

A double take is a quick second look. You might look at something once and not see anything odd. Then you look again and think, "That's impossible!"

You have seen castles before, and you have seen oceans before. But have you ever seen them combined as in painting **A**? In **B**, the fish is a lot bigger than you would expect. Why has the artist changed the proportions this way? What else is strange about picture B?

The Castle in the Pyrenees,
René Magritte
1959. Oil on canvas, 78 3/8 in. X 55 in.

This style of painting is called **Surrealism**. Surrealism mixes and matches possible objects in impossible ways. Separately, the castle and the ocean in picture A are possible. Together, they are just—impossible! Many Surrealist paintings look like dream scenes. Like many dreams, they don't seem to make much sense.

B

Niña con su pescado rojo (Girl and Her Red Fish), **Liliana Wilson Grez**
1993. Acrylic, 48 in. X 36 in.

IN THE STUDIO

MATERIALS

- large sheets of poster board or white paper
- tempera paints
- paintbrushes

Make a Surrealist painting.

Think of one or two real things you see every day. Make a painting that puts these things together in an impossible way. You might "play with reality" by putting the objects in strange places or giving them odd proportions.

Outdoor Spectacles

What is surprising about these sculptures?

Wait a minute! What's a giant spoon holding a cherry doing in a city park? Why are those rusty cars planted in a Texas wheat field?

Each of these sculptures shows a familiar object that has been changed in some way. The spoon in sculpture **A** is almost 50 feet long. The scale of this sculpture makes us stop and take a second look.

A group of artists created sculpture **B** from unusual materials—cars! Why do you think they placed the old cars in the middle of a country landscape? Do you think they were trying to make a point? Why do you think so?

Spoonbridge and Cherry,
Claes Oldenburg and Coosje van Bruggen
1985–88. Stainless steel, painted aluminum, 29 1/2 ft. X 51 1/2 ft. X 13 1/2 ft. Minneapolis Sculpture Garden, Minneapolis, MN.

B *Cadillac Ranch*, Stanley Marsh 3 and the Ant Farm
1974. Car bodies. Near Amarillo, TX, off old Route 66.

IN THE STUDIO

MATERIALS

- soft pencils
- drawing paper
- old newspapers
- thin glue
- boxes, balloons, other unneeded objects
- tempera paints
- paintbrushes

Work by yourself or with a group. Plan a large piece of public art for your community.

1. Think of a special place in your community. Imagine a large sculpture that would fit well there. Draw a sketch of your sculpture and its setting.

2. Make a model of your plan, using papier-mâché. Use a box, a balloon, or some other object for the base of your model. Cover the base with strips of newspaper dipped in thin glue. Let dry, and repeat at least once. Paint your model after it dries again.

Artists use the unexpected to surprise and amuse us.

Did you find any of the artwork in this unit surprising? The work on this page is so surprising that some people do not even call it art. What do *you* think? Are these islands—surrounded by pink fabric—art? Why or why not?

***Surrounded Islands*, Christo and Jeanne-Claude**
1980–1983. Polypropylene fabric,
11 islands. Biscayne Bay, FL.

What Did I Learn?

- **ARTISTS** can surprise us by using unexpected subjects, scale, or media. Find an artwork in this unit that is surprising in one of these ways. Explain why you chose the artwork you did.

- **CHOOSE** an artwork in this unit that fools your eyes and your brain. Why do you think many people enjoy looking at artwork like this?

- **WHICH** artwork in this unit was the most amusing? Explain your opinion.

- **YOU** made some surprising artwork of your own in this unit. How did you use materials, techniques, subjects, or ideas in unexpected ways?

Faraway
drybrush, 1952
copyright 1998 Andrew Wyeth

Harmony and Conflict

How do artists

bring out

different

feelings in

viewers?

Some works of art can make you feel quiet and calm. Some can make you feel tense and excited. How do you feel when you look at *Faraway*?

In this painting, Andrew Wyeth has set his son Jamie in an empty world of grass and twigs. Yet the boy's thoughts seem to be far from empty.

When you look at this painting, can you sense what it would be like to be in the scene? What has the artist done to make you feel this way?

ABOUT ANDREW WYETH

Andrew Wyeth was born in 1917 into a remarkable family. His father, N.C. Wyeth, was one of the greatest illustrators of the day. His son, James, is a celebrated artist, too.

Feelings of Harmony

How can colors and shapes express peaceful feelings?

The beauty of the American West has inspired strong feelings in many artists. What gives these paintings of the West such a feeling of **harmony**, or peace?

In picture **A**, sharp, pointed shapes and lines are repeated in the forest and the mountains. The painter also made the dull shapes of the rocks and the horses alike. Which shapes are alike in picture **B**? Which lines are repeated?

Both artists used yellow and green as important colors. This helps to create harmony, because yellow and green are **analogous colors**. This means that they are next to each other on the color wheel.

Trail Riders,
Thomas Hart Benton
Polymer tempera on canvas,
56 1/8 in. X 74 in.
National Gallery of Art,
Washington, D.C.

Notice how the artists blended the colors. They created **tints** by starting with white and adding color. They created **shades** by starting with color and adding black. Find some tints and shades in each painting. How does this blending add to the feeling of harmony?

B *Squaw Creek Valley*, Florence McClung
1937. Oil on Canvas, 24 1/8 in. X 30 1/8 in.
Dallas Museum of Art, gift of Florence E. McClung

IN THE STUDIO

MATERIALS

- **white paper**
- **watercolors**
- **paintbrushes**

Paint a peaceful scene. Create a feeling of harmony with colors and shapes.

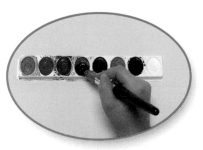

1. **Before painting, choose two or more analogous colors. Then mix tints and shades. To mix tints with watercolors, add extra water to let the white paper show through. To mix shades, start with a color and add black.**

2. **Paint a natural scene. First, paint the large areas, such as sky, water, or forest. Use light colors. Then add details and darker colors. Try to repeat shapes, lines, and textures to add to the harmony.**

A Sense of Excitement

How can a painting show action and excitement?

Picture yourself on a bicycle, zooming down the road in picture **A**. Now imagine tumbling head over heels like the figure in picture **B**. These pictures give viewers a feeling of excitement and movement. How have the artists done this?

In picture A, the orange in the background advances, or seems to jump outward. The blue in the foreground recedes, or seems to move back. This helps to make the hill look very steep. The fact that painting A is long, rather than wide, also makes the hill seem steep.

Nichols Canyon, **David Hockney**
1980. Acrylic on canvas, 84 in. X 60 in.

When complementary colors are put together, they create **contrast**. They can surprise the eyes and make a scene look exciting. Find some complementary colors in each picture.

Curving lines can also create excitement. What curving lines can you find in each picture?

B *Toboggan*, Henri Matisse
1947. Cut and pasted paper, 16 5/8 in. X 25 5/8 in.
Museum of Modern Art, New York.

IN THE STUDIO

MATERIALS

- **soft pencils**
- **colored markers**
- **white paper**

Create a scene that shows movement. Use complementary colors to add contrast and excitement.

1. Think of a scene in which someone or something is moving. Sketch the scene in pencil. Use curves to create a sense of movement.

2. Add color to the sketch. Choose colors that create contrast. You might choose complementary colors from the color wheel, such as orange and blue or violet and yellow.

The Lively Art of David Diaz

Artists can create a sense of movement and excitement on the page.

David Diaz often works with bold, striking colors and sharply cut edges. Look at the colors he used to illustrate Gary Soto's short story "La Bamba." What has David Diaz done to make this title page as exciting as possible?

Artists who illustrate stories face a special challenge. The style and mood of their art must match the style and mood of the story. You can probably guess that "La Bamba" is a lively story. What else can you tell about the story from the art?

▲ **David Diaz**

from Baseball in April and Other Stories

BEST BOOKS FOR YOUNG ADULTS

by Gary Soto

illustrated by David Diaz

WHAT
DO
YOU
THINK
?

▶ **What do you think of when you look at the art for "La Bamba"?**

▶ **How do you think David Diaz's art would look if he had used analogous colors? Explain.**

81

In Balance

How do artists create balance in their works?

Use your finger to draw an imaginary line down the center of picture **A**. Which objects in the left half of the painting have a twin or near-twin in the right half? When an artwork is exactly the same on both sides, it is **symmetrical**. Picture A is almost symmetrical, but not quite. The objects without twins **balance** each other. With your hand, take turns covering up the bookcase and the table with the lamp. Each way, the painting looks lopsided, too heavy on one side or the other.

A **mobile** is a hanging sculpture that moves. Even though mobile **B** is **asymmetrical** (not symmetrical), it is still in balance. This balance can make us feel calm when we watch the mobile's slowly circling shapes.

Victorian Interior, **Horace Pippin**
1945. Oil on canvas, 25 1/4 in. X 30 in.
Metropolitan Museum of Art, New York.

 Untitled, Alexander Calder
National Gallery of Art, Washington, D.C.

IN THE STUDIO

MATERIALS

- branches and twigs
- strong thread or fishing line
- natural objects such as feathers, shells, small rocks, and pieces of wood
- scissors

Create a mobile that is in balance.

1. Use a thick branch for your main crosspiece. Tie thread in the middle of the branch.

2. Hang your branch in a place where you can work on it easily. Tie threads to the ends, and hang objects from them. Your threads can be different lengths. Add and take away threads and objects until your mobile is in balance and moves freely.

Colors in Conflict

How do artists show tension or conflict in their works?

Look at pictures **A** and **B**. How do these pictures make you feel? Then look back at the pictures on pages 76 and 77. Compare the feelings you get when you look at the two pairs of pictures.

Some artists use shapes that do not seem to go together. Picture A is titled *Confusion of Shapes*. Look closely. How

Confusion of Shapes,
Diana Ong

84

did the artist make the shapes look jumbled and confused? What words would you use to describe the way picture A makes you feel?

Some artists use colors that are not seen in nature. These colors, called **arbitrary colors**, can seem as if they don't belong. Surely you have never seen an animal the colors of picture B!

B Student Artwork

IN THE STUDIO

MATERIALS

- oaktag or white paper
- tempera paints
- paintbrushes
- colored paper
- scissors
- glue

Create a collage that shows tension or conflict.

1. Cut colored paper into different shapes. Create shapes that do not seem to belong together.

2. Place your shapes in a mixed-up arrangement on a sheet of oaktag. Then glue them down.

3. Add paint to your collage. Use bold strokes of color.

Art on Parade

Communities organize unique events to celebrate their home, their work, and themselves!

The New Year's Day Tournament of Roses Parade is a great American tradition. Thousands upon thousands of colorful flowers and leaves cover the festive and imaginative floats. In the last few days before the parade, crews work around the clock to add the flowers. Look at this float from the parade. Why might the designer have chosen these colors?

▶ **At work on the _Treasure Island_ float**

86

▲ The *Treasure Island*
float on parade

WHAT
DO
YOU
THINK
?

▶ **What is unusual about an artwork made of flowers?**

▶ **What other celebrations have you seen that included works of art?**

Visual Rhythms

How do artists create rhythm in artwork?

Bop biddly be bop! Your gaze bounces up and down and back and forth when you look at painting **A**. The artist has created a **rhythm** you can see. To do this, he used squares and rectangles of bright, contrasting colors. The **pattern**, or repeated shapes and colors, makes your gaze hop from place to place.

The rhythm is different in painting **B**. The large areas of color and the long curves make your eyes move at a slower pace. What kind of rhythm do you see in painting **C**? Paintings A, B, and C are examples of nonrepresentational art. They do not represent, or show, objects we can recognize. However, they

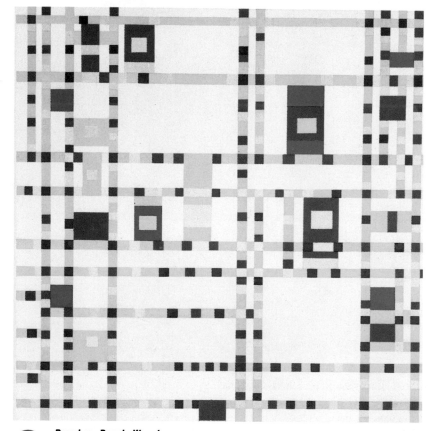

Broadway Boogie Woogie,
Piet Mondrian
1942–43. Oil on canvas, 50 in. X 50 in.
Museum of Modern Art, New York.

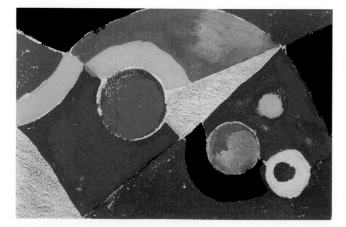

B *Rhythme Colore,*
Sonia Terk Delaunay

can still express feelings and ideas. Look again at painting C. If you were to put music to this painting, which would be the fast parts? Which would be the slow parts? Why?

C *Atmospheric Effects II,*
Alma Woodsey Thomas
1971. Watercolor, 22 in. X 30 in.
National Museum of American Art,
Smithsonian Institution, Washington, D.C.

IN THE STUDIO

MATERIALS

- tempera paints
- dry sponges
- scissors
- white paper

Use repeated colors and shapes to make a print with rhythm.

1. Cut sponges into simple shapes such as circles, squares, and triangles.

2. Dip the shapes into different colors of paint.

3. Dab the shapes onto your paper in a pattern that has its own rhythm. Is your rhythm fast or slow?

Lines of Expression

How can artists show things as *they* see them?

How do you think Vincent van Gogh [van GOH] might have been feeling when he painted this picture? Was he feeling quiet or full of energy? Why do you think so?

Instead of showing a night sky as it really looked, van Gogh showed his feelings about the scene. The huge yellow stars and swirling sky show a world full of movement and light.

The Starry Night, **Vincent van Gogh**
1889. Oil on canvas, 29 in. X 36 1/4 in.
Museum of Modern Art, New York.

Works of art like *The Starry Night* are **expressive**. This means that they express, or show, the artists' feelings. Trace the strong lines around the stars and the moon. Does your gaze move from the right side of the painting to the left, or from left to right? Why? Explain how the lines make you move your eyes.

Van Gogh's expressive works influenced other artists. A later group of artists used colors and shapes as well as lines to express their feelings. These artists are called the **Expressionists**.

You can express your feelings in your artwork, too. Remember that you don't have to show things as they really look. Express yourself!

IN THE STUDIO

MATERIALS

- tempera paints
- paintbrushes
- large sheet of white paper

Paint a landscape or a cityscape.

Think of one of your favorite places in the country or in the city. Paint this scene, using strong lines to express your feelings about it. Try to lead the viewers' gaze from one section of your painting to another.

Art can express feelings of harmony and conflict.

In this unit, you have learned about some of the ways artists show rhythm, pattern, and balance. These techniques, combined with the artist's choice of colors, can have a powerful effect on viewers. Look at this painting by the Spanish artist Pablo Picasso. The artist is showing three musicians. Perhaps they are making music in harmony. However, considering the way the artist has shown them, perhaps they are not.

Three Musicians, **Pablo Picasso**
1921. Oil on canvas, 6 ft. 7 in. X 7 ft. 3 3/4 in. Museum of Modern Art, New York.

What Did I Learn?

- **WHAT** did Pablo Picasso do to create harmony in this painting? What did he do to create conflict?

- **FIND** an artwork in this unit that is like *Three Musicians* in some way. How are the two pieces alike? How are they different?

- **THINK** about the artwork you created in this unit. How did you use rhythm and patterns? How did you use shapes and colors? What other techniques did you use?

- **FIND** an artwork in this unit that shows balance. Explain how the artist created this balance.

***Basket of Light**, **Flor Garduño**
1989.

New Ways to Create

How do artists see things in new and different ways?

Two people can pick up the same camera and point it in the same direction, but they may see very different things through its lens.

The women of Guatemala carried baskets of flowers for centuries before the camera was invented. When photographer Flor Garduño looked through a lens at this young woman, she saw more than a traditional, everyday scene. She saw a work of art. What makes *Basket of Light* more than a snapshot? What makes it a new way of seeing a familiar scene?

ABOUT FLOR GARDUÑO

Flor Garduño was born in Mexico in 1957. She studied photography at the National University in Mexico City. She worked with a master photographer and then set out on an independent career.

Book Art

How did artists long ago decorate books to add beauty and meaning to words?

Pictures **A**, **B**, and **C** show pages from ancient books. All the letters, shapes, and patterns were created by hand.

The printing on picture A is in Latin. Which letters do you recognize? Real gold was used to decorate this page. Pages of this kind are called **illuminated pages** because they look as if they are lit up.

 Illuminated page from
The Book of Lindisfarne
A.D. 700.

B **Illuminated page from the Haggadah**
Circa 1470. Parchment. The Israel Museum, Jerusalem.

The printing on picture B is in Hebrew. Describe some of the patterns and detailed pictures on the page. Is picture B symmetrical? Why or why not?

The printing on picture C is in Persian. What details do you see in and around the illustration? What do you think the writing might be about?

 Old Man and Youth in Landscape, Behzad
Circa 1500. Gold and silver on paper, 3 1/4 in. tall.
Smithsonian Institution, Washington, D.C.

IN THE STUDIO

MATERIALS

- heavy white paper
- colored pencils or fine-tipped marking pens
- tempera paints
- paintbrushes

Create a book cover.

Design a cover for a book, diary, or portfolio. Decorate the title with beautiful patterns and pictures. Try to show what will be inside your cover.

Is Photography Art?

How does photography use technology to make art?

Like paintings, photographs can show feelings and tell stories. Photographers must make many choices in order to create interesting pictures.

Where does your eye go first in picture **A**? This is the **center of interest** in this photograph. Where is the child's face in relation to the picture's **frame**, or edge? Why do you think the photographer made the background look fuzzy or out of **focus**?

Notice the difference between the dark and light areas in picture **B**. This photographer used contrast to separate the sky, the water, and the land. What is the center of interest in picture B? Notice how the viewer's attention is drawn to the center of interest.

 *A Child's Brilliant Smile,* Carol Guzy

IN THE STUDIO

MATERIALS

- light-sensitive sun print paper or photogram kit
- materials such as netting, lace, leaves, and ferns
- pieces of cardboard

Make a photogram. Plan a design that fits well within its frame and that has a clear center of interest.

1. In a darkened room, arrange materials on a piece of light-sensitive paper to form an interesting design. Carefully cover the materials with a piece of cardboard.

2. Carry your design outside, or place it under a desk lamp. Lift the top piece of cardboard for two minutes.

3. Your teacher will help you develop your photogram.

The Photographic Art of George Ancona

Photographers can open doors to other places and other times.

As a teenager, George Ancona visited the *hacienda*, or ranch, owned by his Mexican relatives. He was fascinated by their way of life. Many years later, George Ancona returned to that area as an award-winning photographer. He and author Joan Anderson worked together to re-create a lost place and time. Through Anderson's story and Ancona's highly detailed photos, they showed what life was like for the earliest European settlers in North America. What can you learn about the settlers' lives from George Ancona's photograph on page 101?

▲ **George Ancona**

 A scene from *Spanish Pioneers of the Southwest* by Joan Anderson, photographs by George Ancona

Sculptures Through Time

How have sculptors used similar ideas, but different materials, over the centuries?

Look at sculptures **A**, **B**, and **C**. All three have women as their subjects, but they are different in many ways. Which of these sculptures was made in the twentieth century? What clues did you use to figure this out?

Each sculpture is made of a different material. The oldest one, A, is made of terra-cotta, or clay. B was created out of bronze metal about 2,000 years later. C is made from modern materials.

Long ago, sculptors worked with materials such as clay and stone. Over time, new materials such as metal became available to them. Today sculptors use many different natural and **synthetic**, or human-made, materials. How do you think a sculptor chooses a material?

 Draped, standing woman
Between 776 B.C. and 323 B.C. Terra-cotta.
The Louvre, Paris.

 Queen Mother head
Early sixteenth century. Bronze, 20 in.
National Museum, Lagos, Nigeria.

102

C

Blue Girl on Park Bench, George Segal
1980. Painted plaster and painted aluminum, 51 X 78 X 44 in.
Sidney, Janis Gallery

IN THE STUDIO

MATERIALS

- small, clean milk carton with top cut off
- mixed plaster of Paris
- plastic knife
- aluminum foil
- scissors

Use two different materials to make sculptures. (Or, choose one of these sculptures to make.)

1. Your teacher will mix plaster of Paris and water. Pour the wet plaster into a milk carton. Wait for the plaster to set, and peel away the milk carton. Draw your object on the plaster. Use the plastic knife to scrape away bits of plaster from the column until you have formed the shape you want.

2. Now make a sculpture from aluminum foil. Crumple the foil loosely to make arms and legs. Bend the arms and legs to show movement.

The World of Animation

How do artists bring still pictures to life?

Animation is the art of making still pictures seem to move. An animated movie is made up of many still pictures. Each one is slightly different from the one before. These pictures, or **frames**, are shown on a screen very quickly, one after the other. This creates the illusion of movement.

Picture **A** is a frame from the movie *Pinocchio*, made in 1940. This picture was painted by hand. Picture **B** is from the movie *Toy Story*, made in 1995. Artists used computers to create picture B. How are the frames alike?

A **Frame from *Pinocchio***
1940. The Walt Disney Company.

Artists can create three-dimensional pictures with computer animation. The toys in picture B look like objects you could actually pick up. Picture A looks two-dimensional, like a painting. Yet some people find picture A more interesting. What about you?

 Frame from *Toy Story*
1995. The Walt Disney Company.

IN THE STUDIO

MATERIALS

- **10 or more index cards cut into halves**
- **colored markers**
- **stapler**

Make a flip book that creates the illusion of movement.

1. **Decide what kind of movement you will show. Draw a simple character or object on a card.**

2. **Copy your drawing onto another card, but change the position slightly. Continue to do this on 15 to 20 more cards.**

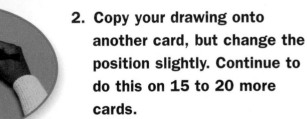

3. **Staple your cards together to make a book. Flip the cards with your thumb and watch your own animation!**

Computer Animator

Karen Kiser *was one of twenty-seven animators who worked on the movie* Toy Story. *As a professional animator, Karen has worked in 2-D, in stop-motion, and in computer animation. Here she talks about her career.*

■ "In 2-D, you draw your characters by hand, changing their shapes with each drawing. In stop-motion, you move a puppet in front of a camera and then take a picture of each change. In computer animation, you manipulate a 3-D model that is programmed into a computer."

▼ **Karen working in stop-motion on the *Gumby* TV series**

▶ Six lively characters from *Toy Story*

■ "I owe a lot to the toys I played with as a child. Dolls and action figures helped shape my imagination as I played out stories in my mind. Most of the animators I know bring their toy collections with them to work."

▲ Karen at work at Pixar Studios, the home of *Toy Story*

■ "As a computer animator, you need to know how to use a computer. However, to make your characters come alive, you need to understand the art of animation. And to make your stories appealing, you need to understand the art of storytelling."

WHAT DO YOU THINK?

▶ Which style of animation would you prefer to work in? Why?

▶ What might be some important qualities for an animator to have?

Celebrations in Stone

How do buildings express a culture's values?

Imagine that you are walking up to a huge stone building such as **A** or **B**. The tall **arch** of the doorway curves over your head. Slender towers point toward the sky. How do you think you would feel?

It took workers hundreds of years to build the Lincoln Cathedral (A). It has thin, pointed towers, called **spires**. A cathedral is a large place of worship for Christians.

Hundreds of years ago, a ruler in India ordered the building in picture B, the Taj Mahal [TAHZH muh•HAHL], built in memory of his wife. It is made of white marble that glows in

 Lincoln Cathedral
Completed circa 1400. 271 ft. tall (central tower).
Lincoln, England.

sunlight or moonlight. The area has two mosques [MAHSKS], which are places of worship for Muslims. The four thin towers at its corners are called **minarets**.

Building A is in the western part of the world, and B is in the eastern part. What feelings do both buildings inspire?

 Taj Mahal
Circa 1632–1648. Marble, 186 ft. square, 120 ft. tall. Agra, India.

IN THE STUDIO

MATERIALS

- large sheets of white paper
- colored pencils
- ruler
- compass

Make a scale drawing of a grand building.

1. Sketch a design for a grand building to celebrate your community.

2. Decide how tall and how long the building will be. Then decide how many feet each inch in your drawing will equal. For instance, 1 inch in your drawing might equal 10 feet in the actual building.

3. You might want to use a ruler and compass to draw your building. Add details with the colored pencils.

Unusual Architecture

Should buildings look very different from their surroundings?

In Lesson 29 you looked at two buildings that were built hundreds of years ago. Pictures **A** and **B** show modern buildings. Each is an art museum designed by a famous architect. What was the first thing you noticed about each building?

Some people, including art critics, disliked these buildings. They said their forms were too different from the older buildings nearby. What do you think?

The stone building in picture A is hundreds of years old. It was once a palace. The pyramid in front is part of the roof

 The Grand Louvre, I. M. Pei
Paris, France.

of a new section that was built underground. The architect wanted to give the museum more space and sunlight. Do you think the glass pyramid was a good solution? Why or why not? What do you think of the museum in picture B?

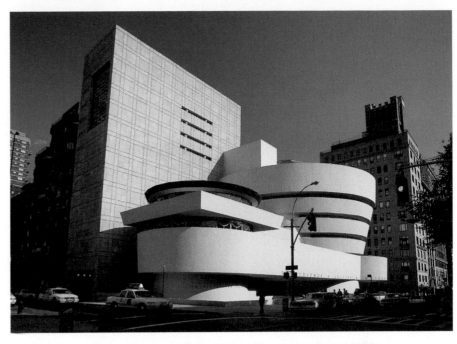

B The Solomon R. Guggenheim Museum, Frank Lloyd Wright
1956–1959. Cast concrete, steel. New York.

IN THE STUDIO

MATERIALS

- foam board or cardboard
- aluminum foil
- paper towel rolls, small boxes, or blocks
- balloons or small balls
- tape or wire
- tempera
- paintbrushes

Think of an unusual building that you would like to build. Make a model of your building.

1. Choose at least five shapes and forms to use in your model. Wrap each one in foil. Arrange your foil-covered shapes and forms into a structure that satisfies you. Attach the pieces with tape or wire.

2. Glue your model to a piece of foam board or cardboard. Paint the base to show what is around your building.

Artists adapt to new technologies.

Think about some of the artwork you saw in this unit. How did the artists find new uses for technology? The artwork on this page shows a spectacular use of technology. *Electronic Superhighway* is composed of television sets, laser disc images, and neon lights. The artist, Nam June Paik, used these materials, along with techniques such as frame and center of interest, to create this unusual work of art.

Electronic Superhighway, **Nam June Paik**
1995. Installation: multiple television monitors, laser disc images, and neon, 15 ft. X 32 ft.

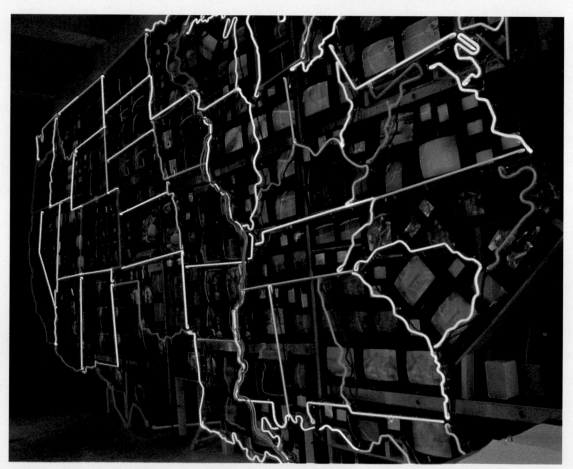

What Did I Learn?

- **THINK** about the artwork you created in this unit. How did you use a technique or a material in a new way?

- **LOOK** back through the unit. Find examples of frame and center of interest in the art. Compare how different artists used these techniques.

- **FIND** two artworks in this unit that you like. Tell how you think the artists who made these were especially creative.

- **NAME** three kinds of materials used by the artists in this unit. How did the artists find new ways of seeing and doing things with these materials?

Moses, Michelangelo
Circa 1513–1515. Marble, approximately 8 ft. 4 in. high.
San Pietro in Vincoli, Rome.

Heritage and Change

How do artists preserve the heritage of a culture?

All cultures celebrate their religion and their heritage through art. Michelangelo (my•kuhl•AN•juh•loh) is thought to be one of the greatest artists of the Western world. This statue of Moses is one of his masterpieces. What can you tell about Moses simply by looking at Michelangelo's statue?

Michelangelo's sculptures and paintings can be seen in many great churches in Italy. In his work, Michelangelo not only preserved the stories of the past, he also gave them to future generations.

ABOUT MICHELANGELO

Michelangelo Buonarroti was born in 1475 in Caprese, Italy. At 13, he became an artist's apprentice in Florence and soon earned the support of the rich and art-loving Medici family.

Stories on Walls

How can artists tell stories with pictures?

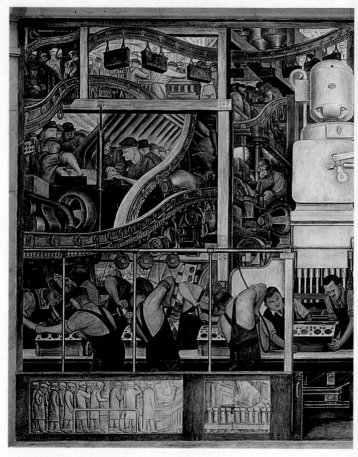

Murals are large paintings done on walls. Artists often paint murals to tell stories about people. Like a story in a book, a mural can express a **theme**, or main idea.

Diego Rivera, a Mexican artist, is famous for his murals about Mexican history and culture. Rivera was hired to paint this mural for the city of Detroit, Michigan. It shows workers in one of the many automobile factories. There is so much going on in this noisy place! Everyone seems to be working hard and cooperating. Notice the conveyor belts that snake through the factory. The artist wanted viewers to see the textures and patterns of the machines. He wanted us to feel the rhythm of the men working with machines.

Do you think the artist respected these workers? Why or why not?

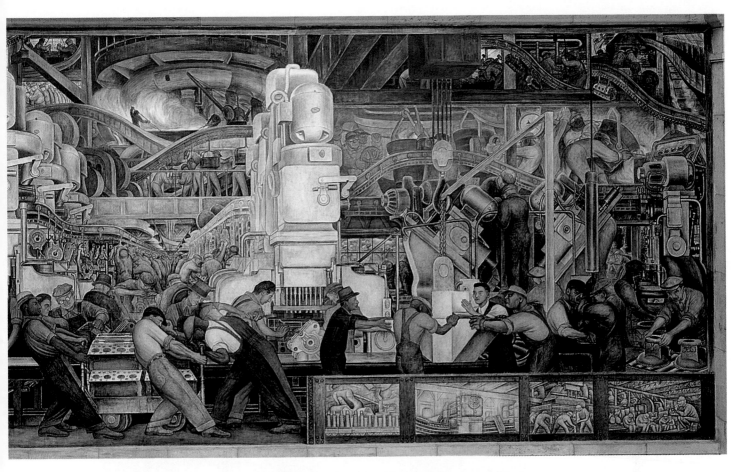

 Detroit Industry, **North Wall (detail), Diego M. Rivera**
1932–33. Detroit Institute of Arts, Detroit.

IN THE STUDIO

MATERIALS

- tempera paints
- paintbrushes
- long sheet of butcher paper

Create a mural that tells a story.

With your classmates, plan a mural that tells a story about your school or community. Include a theme in your mural. Begin with a small-scale drawing. Use pencils to sketch your drawing onto butcher paper. Then paint your mural with tempera paints.

Centuries in Clay

How do artists learn from each other?

The pottery in **A** was made in China about 1,000 years ago. The designs were attached to the pot with **slip**, a mixture of water and clay.

The vase in **B** was also made in China, about 700 years ago. By that time, Chinese potters had learned to use **porcelain**, a hard, pure clay. Some of the designs on B were attached with slip. Others were cut, or **incised**, into the clay.

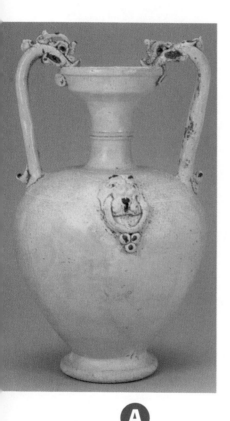

White earthenware urn, Tang Dynasty
Circa 600–900. Earthenware, 14 1/2 in.

B **Porcelain vase, Chinese**
Circa 1300. Porcelain.

The pottery in **C** was made in England about 140 years ago. The potter who made C had learned from older Chinese vases like A and B. How is C like the Chinese vases? How is it different?

 Copeland Vase, painted by Hürton
1862. Porcelain, 27 1/2 in.

IN THE STUDIO

MATERIALS

- clay
- rolling pin
- sponge
- tools such as toothpicks and plastic knives

Make a slab pot. Add a design that fits its purpose.

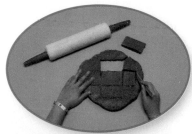

1. Roll out a ball of clay until it is about half an inch thick. Cut out one piece to make the bottom of the pot and four pieces to make the sides.

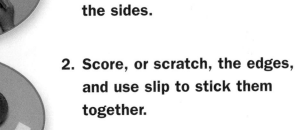

2. Score, or scratch, the edges, and use slip to stick them together.

3. Use a tool to decorate the outside of the pot. Think about how you will use your pot. Decide what kind of design would fit that purpose.

African Adobe Architecture

Architecture around the world reflects the spirit of the people and the resources of the land.

People of all cultures and in all countries create beautiful buildings. Many beautiful buildings, such as churches and mosques, are created as places of worship.

▼ **The Great Mosque of Djenné, Mali**

The beautiful mosques on these pages rise up from the sprawling Sahara desert in northern Africa. Their architects and builders constructed them from adobe, a desert clay. The Great Mosque at Djenné [jen•AY] is one of the largest adobe buildings ever made. The Mosque at Bobo Dioulasso [dyoo•LASS•oh] was made from desert clay painted with lime.

Mosque at Bobo Dioulasso, Burkina Faso ▼

WHAT
DO
YOU
THINK
?

▶ **What might these mosques tell you about the people who designed them?**

▶ **How are the two mosques like buildings you have seen? How are they different?**

A Timeless Art

How do artists help keep traditions alive?

Have your grandparents or older relatives ever told you stories about their childhoods? Stories of that kind help us learn about earlier times. They can also help us keep important traditions alive.

Pablita Velarde [pab•LEET•uh vel•AHR•day] is a Native American artist. She is a member of the Pueblo culture of the American Southwest. She paints pictures based on her childhood memories and the stories her grandparents told her. Look at the scene in picture **A**. Notice the rugs, blankets, and belts in the room. **Weaving** is the process of

Her First Dance,
Pablita Velarde
1953. 16 3/4 in. X 15 in.
Denver Art Museum.

turning thread or yarn into cloth. For hundreds of years, weaving has been an important part of the Pueblo heritage.

Look at the woven belt in picture **B**. Native American weavers used wool to make belts such as this one. What patterns can you find in it?

B *Iowa Sash*, **Nebraska**
Circa 1880. Wool yarn, 79 X 1/4 in.
Museum of the American Indian.

IN THE STUDIO

MATERIALS

- **thin yarn, various colors**
- **straws (5)**
- **stirrer straws**
- **scissors**

Weave a bookmark. Use analogous colors.

1. Cut five pieces of yarn, each two feet long. Fold the pieces in half. Using a stirrer, push each piece of yarn through a straw. Tie each pair of loose ends together. Thread another piece of yarn through the loops of the folded ends and tie them loosely together.

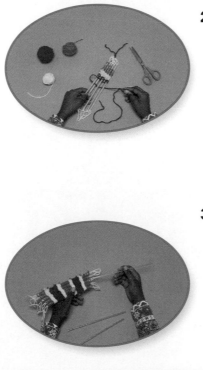

2. Take another piece of yarn and tie it around one of the outer straws. Weave the yarn over and under each straw to form rows. When you want to change to a different color, tie the new color to the end of the preceding color. Continue weaving.

3. Weave all the way down to the folded end. Then untie the folded ends and pull off the straws. Finish your bookmark by cutting the ends into even lengths of fringe.

Patchwork Art

How did quilting become an art form?

New blankets were expensive and hard to come by in early America. Pioneer women sewed scraps of cloth together to make **quilts** such as the one in picture **A**. All the work was done by hand. Groups of women gathered at events called quilting bees to help each other sew. A quilt, however, was not just a blanket. It was a work of art.

Patchwork quilting is a form of collage. It combines different materials and designs in one artwork. Today artists use patchwork quilting techniques to make beautiful works of art as shown in picture **B**.

Notice the geometric patterns in quilts A and B. In both quilts, shapes are repeated to create strong designs. Can you identify some of these designs?

Album Quilt, **friends and relatives of Mary Brown Turner**
Begun in 1846. Appliquéd and quilted cotton, 83 3/8 in. X 85 in.
Metropolitan Museum of Art, New York.

Heartland, Miriam Schapiro
1985. Fabric, 85 in. X 94 in.
Orlando Museum of Art, Orlando, FL.

IN THE STUDIO

MATERIALS

- scraps of cloth
- needles and thread or safety pins
- scissors
- trim such as sequins and lace
- fabric paint or markers

Make your own quilt square. With your classmates, make a patchwork wall hanging.

1. Work with your classmates to plan the size, shape, colors, and design of your wall hanging.

2. Decorate your own cloth square with fancy trim and fabric paint.

3. Have a classroom quilting bee! Sew or pin together all of the squares.

THE ARTRAIN

It's a bird! It's a plane! It's a museum on wheels called the Artrain!

Not every community has a museum people can visit. However, for any community that has railroad tracks, there is a museum that can visit people. In fact, the Artrain has been visiting people all over the United States since 1971. What are some reasons why a train makes a good museum?

▼ The Artrain on the move

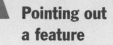

▲ Pointing out a feature

◀ Taking a closer look

WHAT DO YOU THINK?

▶ If you could choose art for the Artrain, what would it be? Why?

▶ Why might it be important for people in different parts of the United States to view the same art?

Artwork to Wear

How do artists turn raw materials into jewelry?

Long ago, people wore jewelry as a sign of power and wealth. Is jewelry worn for the same reasons today? What are some other reasons people wear jewelry?

The gold and gemstone headdress in picture **A** was found in the tomb of an ancient king. It was made by hand more than 4,000 years ago!

The jewelry in picture **B** was crafted in Spain about 300 years ago. Emeralds, diamonds, enamel, and gold were used to create the delicate **ornamentation**, or decoration. Can you see the repeated flower shapes?

A
Mesopotamian chaplet of gold leaves
Circa 2600–2500 B.C. Gold, lapis lazuli, and carnelian, 15 1/8 in.
The Metropolitan Museum of Art.

B **Spanish corsage ornament**
Beginning of the eighteenth century. Gold, enamel, emeralds, and diamonds.
Victoria & Albert Museum, London.

A modern Native American artist made the necklace in picture **C** from a shell. He decorated it with turquoise, mother-of-pearl, and black stone. Notice the strong geometric patterns on this necklace. Why do you think each artist used the materials he or she did?

 Southwestern United States shell and turquoise necklace, "Ca Win" Jimmy Calabaza
1984. Spondylus shell, inlaid with mother-of-pearl, jet, and turquoise.

IN THE STUDIO

MATERIALS

- **wire or string**
- **magazines**
- **glue**
- **scissors**
- **other necklace items such as pasta and washers**

Create your own beads. Use them to make a bead necklace.

1. Cut brightly colored magazine pages into 1-inch strips.

2. Spread glue on one strip at a time. Fold one end of the strip around a pencil and gently roll it into a tight tube. Remove the pencil and let the glue dry. Repeat for other strips.

3. String the beads on wire or strong string. Think of creative items to use as spacers as you string the other necklace items in a pattern.

Faces from Folk Art

Why is mask-making popular all around the world?

A **Jaguar mask**
About 1960. Painted wood,
9¹/₂ in. Mexico.

When do people wear masks? Why do they wear them? In some cultures, masks are worn to represent story characters or important people. In many places the tradition of mask-making is passed from one generation of **folk artists** to the next. These artists learn the craft by watching their elders.

Picture **A** shows a jaguar mask from Mexico. It is worn in dances in which the jaguar is a character. In Mexico, the jaguar is a traditional symbol of courage and strength.

Mask **B** was made for an actor in a Japanese play. Masks for these plays have been made for hundreds of years. Every detail follows rules that have been handed down through generations.

Nō mask of Okina, Ujiharu Nagasawa
Twentieth century. 7 in. tall.

Mask **C** shows the mother of an African king. The king's mother, called the *iyoba*, had a special place of honor in the African kingdom of Benin.

Mask representing an iyoba
Circa 1550. Ivory, iron, copper,
9³/₈ in. tall. Benin.

IN THE STUDIO

Create a mask. You may want to work in one of the styles shown in this lesson or in a style that reflects your own heritage.

1. **Decide which style of mask you want to make. Draw an outline of your mask on tagboard.**

2. **Cut out two holes for the eyes and a hole for the mouth. Use paper scraps and other materials to make the ears, nose, hair, and other features. Glue them to the mask.**

3. **Paint your mask. When it is dry, punch holes on both sides of the face so you can attach an elastic band across the back. Try it on!**

Artists preserve and build upon their heritages.

Art is not always the brushstrokes of a painting or the lines of a statue. Art can be the movements of dancers, the playing of musicians, and so on. The artists of Ballet Folklórico (folk dance) celebrate traditional Mexican forms of dance and music. They use them in lively new combinations. How is their creation like a painting?

Ballet Folklórico Dancers
from McAllen, Texas, at Texas
Folklife Festival in San Antonio.

What Did I Learn?

- **THE** artistic traditions of many cultures were represented in this unit. Which tradition was the most interesting to you? Explain your choice.

- **IDENTIFY** two artworks in this unit that had cultural themes or that told stories about a culture.

- **YOU** made some traditional artwork of your own in this unit. How did you use theme and storytelling in your artwork?

- **WHICH** artists in this unit wanted to preserve their heritage? Which artists were interested in adding new things to their heritage?

Listen carefully when your teacher tells how to use art materials.

Wear a smock to keep your school clothes clean.

Use the kind of markers and inks that will not stain your clothes.

Use tools carefully. Hold sharp objects so that they cannot hurt you or others. Wear safety glasses if something could get in your eyes.

Check labels on materials before you use them. Look for the word *nontoxic*, which means "not poisonous."

Cover your skin if you have a cut or scratch. Some art materials, such as clay, can make cuts sting.

Show respect for other students. Walk carefully around their work. Never touch classmates' work without asking first.

Keep your area clean and neat. Clean up spills right away so no one will fall. Put materials back when you finish with them.

Tell your teacher if you have allergies or breathing problems. Some people are allergic to the kinds of dust in some art materials.

Always wash your hands after using art materials.

Trying Ways to Draw

There are lots of ways to draw. You can draw quickly to show action, or you can draw something very carefully to show just how it looks to you. Try to draw every day. Keep your drawings in your sketchbook so you can see how your drawing changes.

Here are some ideas for drawing. To start, get out your sketchbook or a sheet of paper and some pencils.

GESTURE DRAWING

Gesture drawing is used to show movement or action instead of details. Look at the two pictures of a baseball player. The drawing on the left shows details of the player's uniform, but the gesture drawing catches the feeling of movement as the player swings the bat.

Find some photographs of people or animals in action. Make gesture drawings of them. Draw quickly. Don't try to show details.

Then make some gesture drawings while watching a sporting event. Catch the movement, not the details. Make your sketches quick and lively.

136

CONTOUR DRAWING

Look closely at the lines and shapes in this photograph. The lines that go around shapes are called contours. Use your finger to trace around the outlines of the objects in this picture. Trace the lines inside the shapes too. In a contour drawing, you draw all the lines, edges, and shapes.

Blind contour drawing is a way to learn to look closely at what you are drawing. Choose a simple object, like a leaf. Draw the object without looking at your paper. Move your pencil as your eyes slowly follow the contours. Don't worry if your drawing doesn't look much like the object. Remember, you are using blind contour drawing to learn how to look at things carefully, the way an artist does.

Now try a continuous contour drawing. Draw something simple, like a chair. This time, look back and forth between the object and your paper. Work more quickly. Draw all the edges and shapes without lifting your pencil off the paper. Your drawing will look loose and lively.

Now try making contour drawings of another object, such as a shoe. Lift your pencil whenever you want to. When you feel ready, try a contour drawing of a person.

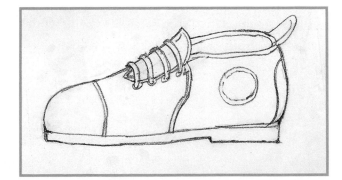

TONAL DRAWING

You can show the shape of something without using contour lines. Look at the photograph of the steps. Notice which areas are dark and which are light. (The darkness or lightness of a color is its **value**.) Now look at the drawing of the steps. It was made with only tones, or **shades**. Even without contour lines, you can tell what the object is.

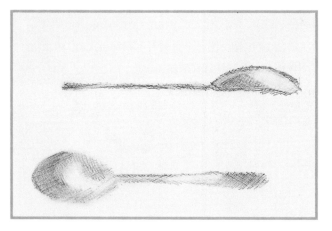

Experiment with your pencils. Try making a series of lines that go from light values to dark values. Try smudging some of the lines together with your fingers. Then use an eraser to lighten some of the smudges. The light areas are called **highlights**. Try this with **cross-hatching** or another small **pattern**.

Try a tonal drawing of a simple object like a spoon. Look at the object closely. Use a flashlight to change the lighting on the spoon. Watch what happens to the highlights as you move the flashlight. Now draw what you see. Show the highlights by erasing the shading where the light looks brightest. Move the flashlight to a different position and make another tonal drawing. Can you tell that the light is coming from a different direction in each drawing?

Try combining tonal drawing with contour drawing. Start by making a tonal drawing of something with an interesting shape, like a book bag. Look at it carefully to see the tones of dark and light.

Then look at the object again to see its contours. Add the outline, edges, and other contour lines.

You might prefer to start with a contour drawing. Be sure you draw the outline of each shape and detail. Then add tones with shading or patterns.

DID YOU PREFER to start with shading or with contours? Either way is fine.

Experimenting with Paint

Working with colors is always fun. Experimenting with paints will help you learn about how artists use color and how you can use it in your artwork.

These are some things you should have when you paint: old newspapers to cover your work area, an old shirt to cover your clothes, tempera paints or watercolors, old dishes or plastic egg cartons for mixing paint, paper, paintbrushes, a jar or bowl of water, and paper towels.

TEMPERA PAINTS

Tempera paints are water-based, so they are easy to clean up. The colors are bright and easy to mix.

● GETTING STARTED

Start experimenting by dipping your paintbrush into one color. Try different kinds of **brushstrokes**. Try painting with lots of paint on the brush and with the brush almost dry. (You can dry the paintbrush by wiping it across a paper towel.) Twist the paintbrush on the paper and roll it, press it, or dab it.

Now clean your brush and use a different color to make a heavy brushstroke. Use a craft stick or another tool to draw a pattern in it.

Make a pattern or a picture on a fresh sheet of paper. Use some of these methods of painting. Try using a different color for each method.

● MIXING COLORS

Even if you have only a few colors of tempera paints, you can mix them to make almost any color you want. An old saucer makes a good palette for mixing paint. You can also use a plastic egg carton. Try using different amounts of the same colors.

To make darker values of colors (shades), add black. Add colors to white to make lighter values (**tints**). See how many shades and tints of a single color you can make. Try starting with a color you have mixed from two colors.

TECHNIQUES TO TRY

Pointillism is a technique that makes the viewer's eyes mix the colors. Start with two colors. Make many small dots of one color very close together. About half an inch away, make many small dots of the other color. In between, make many small dots of each color without letting the dots touch. Stand back from your paper. What happens to the colors as your eyes move across them?

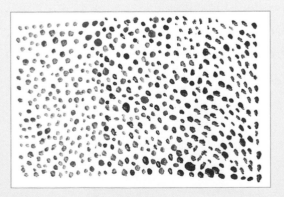

Impasto is a technique that uses a thick mixture of paint and wheat paste. Put some wheat paste in a small bowl. Stir in some paint. Spread some of the mixture on a small piece of cardboard. Experiment with tools such as a toothpick, a plastic fork, or a comb to make textures in the impasto. Then mix more colors. Use them to make an impasto picture or design.

WATERCOLORS

Watercolors usually come in little dry cakes. You have to add the water!
So keep a jar of clean water and some paper towels nearby as you paint.
Use paper that is made for watercolors.

● GETTING STARTED

First put a few drops of water on each cake of paint. To start experimenting with watercolors, dip your paintbrush in water and then dab it in one of the colors. Try some brushstrokes. Watercolors are transparent. Since you can see through them, the color on your paper will never be as dark as the color of the cake. Use different amounts of water. What happens to the color when you use a lot of water?

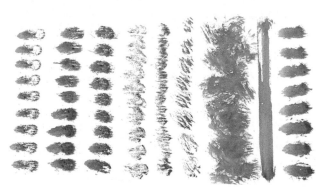

Now rinse your brush in the water and use another color. Try different kinds of brush-strokes—thick and thin, squiggles and waves, dots and blobs. Change colors often.

Try using one color on top of a different color that is already dry. Work quickly to keep the colors clear. If your brushstrokes are too slow, the colors can get muddy. If you want part of your painting to be white, don't paint that part. The white comes from the color of the paper.

● MIXING COLORS

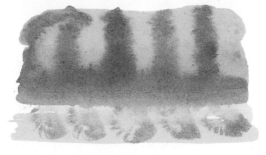

Experiment with mixing watercolors right on your paper. Try painting with a very wet brush over a dry color. Try a wet color on or just touching another wet color. Try three colors together.

You can also mix colors on your paintbrush. Dip your brush into one color and then another before you paint. Try it with green and yellow. Clean your paintbrush and try some other combinations. To clean any paint cakes that you have used for mixing, just wipe them with a paper towel.

TECHNIQUES TO TRY

Try making a wash. Start with a stripe of dark blue. Then clean your paintbrush and get it very wet. Use it to "wash" the color down the page. (You can do this with a wide brush or a sponge, too.) Also try wetting all of one side of the paper. Then brush a stroke of color across it and let the color spread. Try two or three color washes together. For a special effect, sprinkle salt onto a wet wash.

Try using tempera paints and watercolors together. Start with a two-color watercolor wash. Let it dry. Then use several kinds of brushstrokes to paint a design on the wash with one color of tempera. How does the background color change the way the tempera color looks?

Remember these techniques when you paint designs or pictures. Be sure to clean your paintbrushes and work area when you have finished.

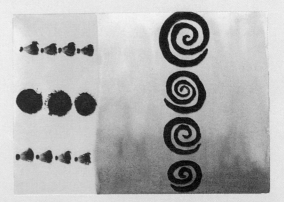

Working with Clay

Clay is a special kind of earth that holds together and is easy to shape when it is mixed with water. Water-based clays can be fired, or heated at a high temperature, or just left in the air to dry until hard.

To make an object with clay, work on a clean, dry surface. (A brown paper bag makes a good work surface.) Have some water handy to work into the clay a few drops at a time if it starts to dry out. When you are not working with it, store clay in a plastic bag to keep it from drying out.

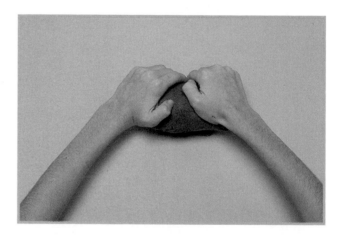

You can use an assortment of tools. To help you shape your clay or to add texture or designs to something you make out of clay, you can use a plastic knife and fork, a rolling pin, keys, a comb, a pencil, a piece of burlap, and other tools.

Start working with a piece of clay by making sure it has no air bubbles in it. Press it down, fold it over, and press it down again. This process is called kneading.

MODELING

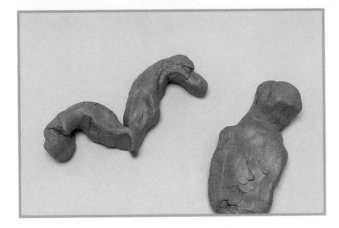

Try making different forms with your clay.
If one of your forms reminds you of an animal or a person, continue to model, or shape, the form by pinching and pulling the clay.

To join shaped pieces, score, or make lines in, the clay surfaces, and wet them.
Or you can coat the surfaces with **slip**, which is clay mixed with water until it is like cream. Then press the surfaces together and smooth the seams.

To make a bigger form, try to model clay around tubes or crumpled newspaper.
Try adding patterns, textures, or details to your figure. Experiment with your tools. Press things into the clay and lift them off. Brush a key across the clay. Try making patterns by combining the shapes made by your tools. Press textured material like burlap into your clay, lift it off, and add designs. If you change your mind, smooth the clay with your fingers and try something else.

Roll your clay out flat, between a quarter-inch and a half-inch thick. If it is soft, you can shape it by draping it over something like a bowl or crumpled paper.

To make a slab box, roll your clay out flat. Cut two squares the same size with a plastic knife. One square will be the bottom of your box, and the other will be the top. To make the sides, cut four rectangles the same length as the square. (Later you can try this with other shapes.)

Score the edges and then let the pieces dry until they feel like leather. Join the pieces together with slip. Then smooth the seams with your fingers.

USING COILS

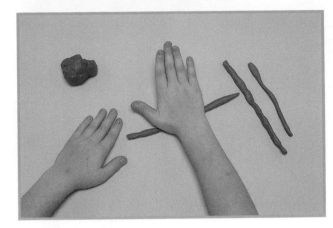

To make a coil pot, roll pieces of clay against a hard surface. Use your whole hand to make long clay ropes.

Make the bottom of your pot by coiling together one or more ropes of clay. Smooth the coils with your fingers. To start the sides, place a rope of clay around the edge of the bottom. Keep attaching ropes and continue the coiling until your pot is as high as you want it. Smooth the inside as you work. You may smooth the outside or let the coils show.

MAKING A CLAY RELIEF

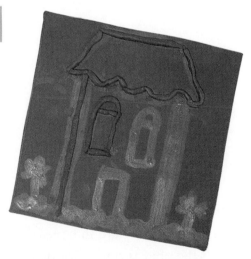

A relief is a sculpture raised from a surface. To make a relief out of clay, start with a slab of any shape. Draw a simple design on the clay, using a brush dipped in slip. Roll some very thin coils. Apply the thin coils to the lines of the design.

You can also make small balls of clay and use slip to add them to the design. Try using some of your other tools to add texture to your design.

Exploring Printmaking

When you make a print, you transfer color from one object to another. If you have ever left a muddy footprint on a clean floor, you know what a print is. Here are some printmaking ideas to try.

COLLOGRAPH PRINTS

A collograph is a combination of a **collage** and a print. To make a collograph, you will need cardboard, glue, paper, newspapers, a brayer (a roller for printing), printing ink, a flat tray such as an old cookie sheet, and some paper towels or sponges. You will also need some thin objects to include in the collage. Try things like these: old keys, string, lace, paper clips, buttons, shells, and burlap.

Spread glue on the cardboard. Arrange several objects on the cardboard in a pleasing design. Press the objects down firmly. Let the glue dry.

Prepare your ink while the collage is drying. Place a small amount of ink on your cookie sheet. Roll the brayer through the ink until it is evenly coated. Gently run the brayer over the collage. Most of the ink should be on the objects.

Now press a piece of paper onto the inked collage. Gently rub the paper. Peel off the paper and let the ink dry. You've made a collograph!

MULTICOLOR PRINTS

You can use different colors of tempera paint to make a multicolor print with repeated patterns. You will need a plastic foam tray (such as a meat tray), cardboard, scissors, glue, paper, water, tempera paint, and a paintbrush.

First cut out some interesting shapes from the plastic foam tray. Carve or poke holes and lines into the shapes. Arrange the pieces on the cardboard to make an interesting design. Glue down the pieces.

When the glue is dry, paint the pieces with different colors of tempera paint. Try not to get paint on the cardboard.

While the paint is wet, place a sheet of paper on top of your design. Gently rub the paper, and peel it off carefully. Let the paint dry. Wipe the shapes dry, and paint them again with different colors. Print the same paper again, but turn it so that the designs and colors overlap.

TRY DIFFERENT COLORS, paper, and objects to make prints.

Displaying Your Artwork

Displaying your artwork is a good way to share it. Here are some ways to make your artwork look its best.

DISPLAYING ART PRINTS

Select several pictures that go together well. Line them up along a wall or on the floor. Try grouping the pictures in different ways. Choose an arrangement that you like. Attach a strong string across a wall. Use clothespins or paper clips to hang your pictures on the string.

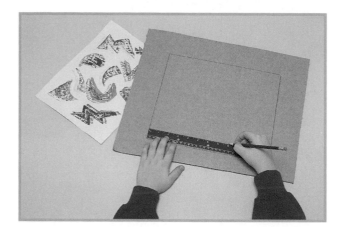

Frame your picture. Use a piece of cardboard that is longer and wider than the art. Draw a rectangle on the cardboard that is larger than your picture. Have an adult cut out the rectangle. Then decorate your frame. Choose colors and textures that look good with your picture. You can paint the frame or use a stamp print design. You can add texture by gluing on strips of cardboard or rows of buttons.

Mount your picture. Glue the corners to a piece of cardboard the same size as the frame. Measure carefully to be sure you get your picture in the center. Then glue the frame to the mounting. Tape a loop of thread on the back. Hang up your framed work.

DISPLAYING SCULPTURES

To display your clay pieces or sculptures, find a location where your work will be safe from harm. Look for a display area where people won't bump into your exhibit or damage your work.

Select several clay pieces or sculptures that go together well. Try grouping them in different ways. Place some of the smaller objects on boxes. Choose an arrangement that you like. Tape any boxes to the table.

Select a large tablecloth or piece of fabric to drape over the table. Pick a plain cloth that looks good with your artwork. Place your artwork back on the table. Try adding a few interesting folds in the cloth near your pieces.

NOW INVITE your friends and family over to see your work!

ELEMENTS & PRINCIPLES

Have you ever thought of art as a language?

Art communicates feelings, stories, and ideas. The **elements of art and principles of design** are like the words and sentences of the language of art. They are the tools artists use to communicate.

This section will show you the elements and principles. You may want to return to this section now and then to help you think about art.

As you learn more about the elements and principles, try to notice line, shape, and pattern all around you. Think about how artists, including yourself, use color, balance, and texture. Learn to look for and use the language of art.

Line

horizontal

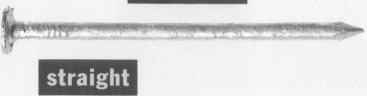

straight

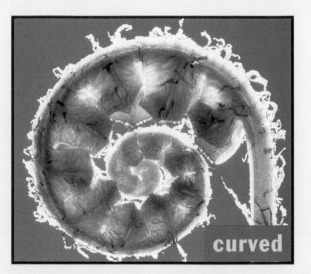

curved

diagonal

zigzag

vertical

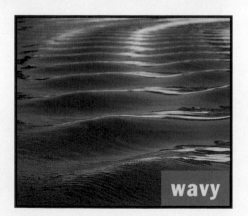

wavy

ELEMENTS
Texture

soft

rough

silky

smooth

bumpy

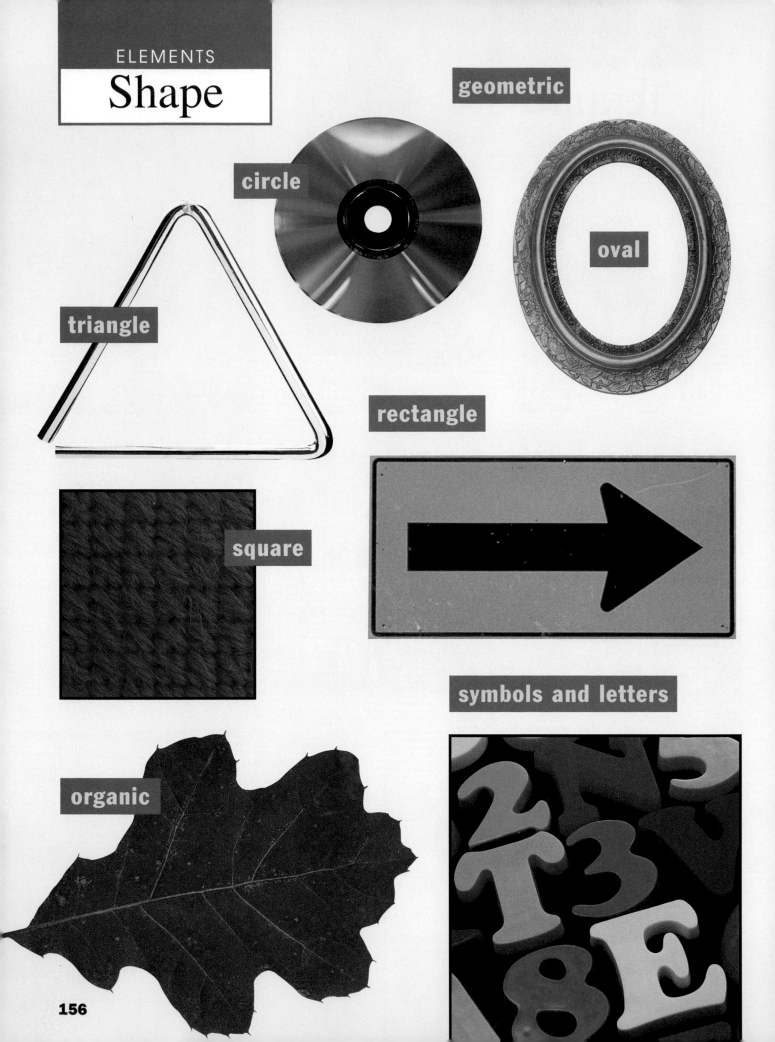

ELEMENTS
Shape

geometric

circle

triangle

oval

rectangle

square

symbols and letters

organic

156

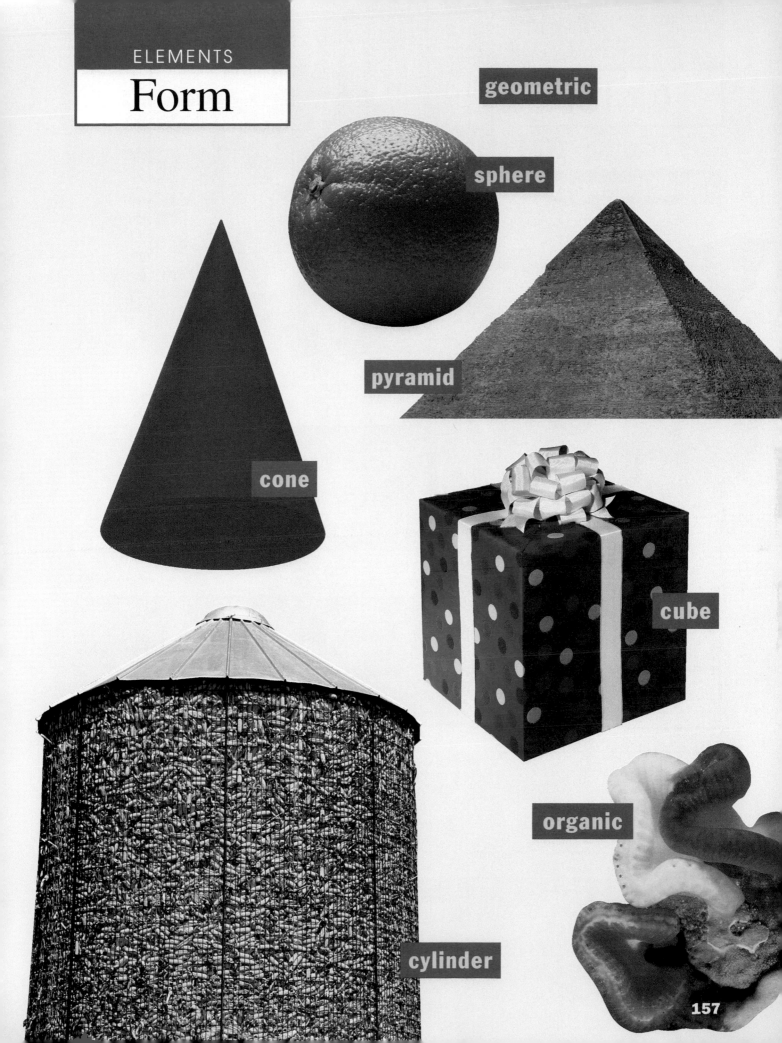

ELEMENTS
Form

geometric

sphere

pyramid

cone

cube

cylinder

organic

157

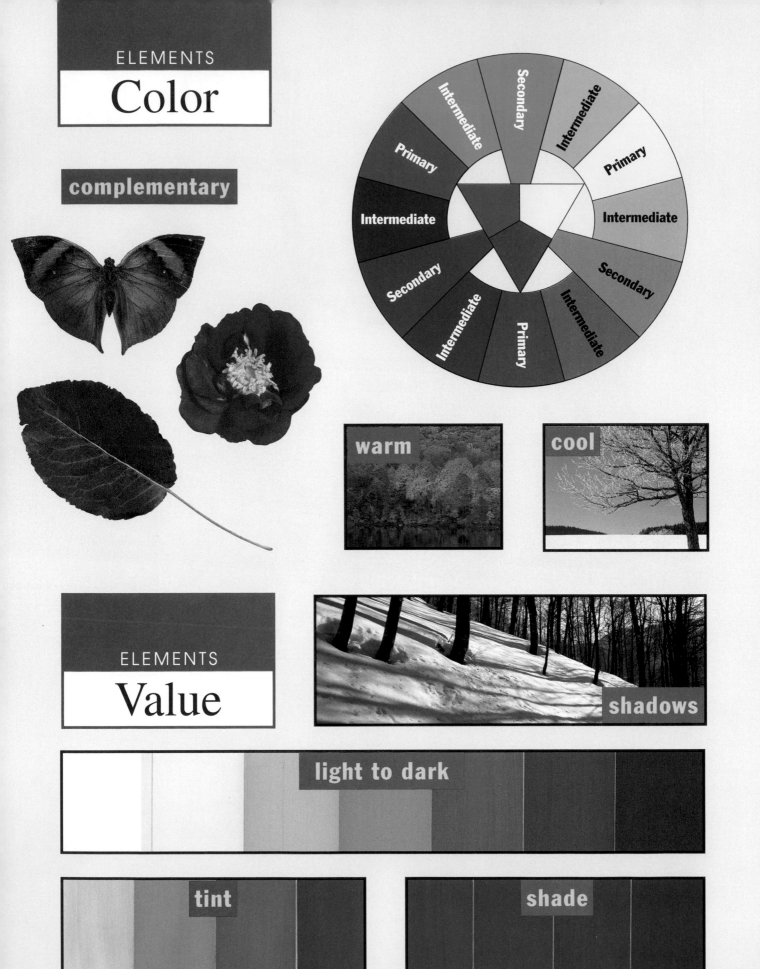

ELEMENTS
Color

complementary

Secondary
Intermediate
Primary
Intermediate
Primary
Intermediate
Secondary
Intermediate
Primary
Intermediate
Secondary
Intermediate

warm

cool

ELEMENTS
Value

shadows

light to dark

tint

shade

Space

positive, negative

proportion

background

middle ground

foreground

point of view

eye level

worm's eye

bird's eye

Unity

repeated lines, textures, colors, shapes, forms

Variety

different lines, textures, colors, shapes, forms

Emphasis

PRINCIPLES
Movement and Rhythm

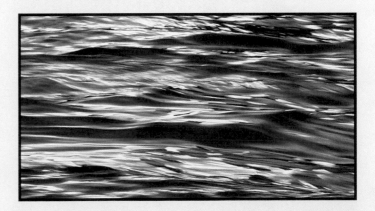

163

Proportion

Balance

asymmetrical

symmetrical

physical balance

GALLERY OF ARTISTS

George Ancona
(1929–) United States, photographer. Ancona was born in Coney Island, New York. After high school, he attended the Academy of San Carlos in Mexico. His work has since been published nationwide in magazines and children's books. **pages 100–101**

Richard Anuszkiewicz
[a•nuh•SKAY•vich]
(1930–) United States, painter. Anuszkiewicz, whose parents came to the United States from Poland, was born in Erie, Pennsylvania. He was one of the first American painters to create the effect of vibration on a flat surface. He was also a pioneer of using the technique of mixing colors optically. **page 59**

Frédéric-Auguste Bartholdi [bar•TOHL•dee] (1834–1904) France, sculptor. Bartholdi, who designed the Statue of Liberty, may have modeled Liberty's face after his mother's. Bartholdi created many huge patriotic sculptures. His style was influenced by the monuments of ancient Egypt. **page 44**

Barbara Bash United States, illustrator. Bash began her publishing career as an artist specializing in calligraphy and botanical illustration. She is now an award-winning author and illustrator of books about nature for young people. **pages 20–21**

Behzad (c. 1455 – c. 1536) Persia, painter. Behzad was an important Persian painter whose style had a strong influence on Persian Islamic painting. He was an orphan who was raised by the painter Mirak Naqqash. In 1522 he was placed in charge of the royal library and made responsible for producing its illuminated and illustrated manuscripts. **page 97**

Thomas Hart Benton
(1889–1975) United States, painter. Benton was born in Missouri and studied at the Art Institute of Chicago as well as in Paris. He painted a number of murals, including those on the walls of the Lounge in the Capitol Building in Washington, D.C. He was thought of as a Regionalist. **page 76**

Selma Burke (1900–1995) United States, sculptor. Burke, one of ten children, was born in Mooresville, North Carolina. She studied to be a nurse but decided to pursue a career in art. She gained national fame in 1945 when she was commissioned to create a plaque of President Franklin Delano Roosevelt. This same image was used on the Roosevelt dime. **page 34**

Alexander Calder (1898–1976) United States, sculptor, painter. Calder was born in Lawnton, Pennsylvania, and studied at the Art Students League in New York. He had his first one-person show at a gallery in New York in 1926. Calder's work is owned by museums around the world. **pages 30, 83**

Mary Cassatt [kuh•SAT] (1844–1926) United States, painter. Cassatt was born in Allegheny City, Pennsylvania, to wealthy parents. She studied at the Pennsylvania Academy of Fine Arts and traveled to Europe often before finally moving there in 1874. She lived in France for the rest of her life. **page 28**

Christo (1935–) Bulgaria, sculptor. Christo studied at the Fine Arts Academy in Sofia, Bulgaria. In 1960, he began wrapping found objects—such as bottles, cans, and even cars— using cloth and plastic and tying them with string. Christo works with his wife, Jeanne-Claude. Their wrapped objects include monuments, bridges, and buildings. **page 72**

Thomas Cole (1801–1848) United States, painter. When Cole was young, he hiked around and sketched the Hudson River valley and areas around the Catskill and Adirondack mountains. He was one of the first artists to capture the spacious feeling of the wilderness, and he had a strong influence on American landscape painting of the 1800s. **page 22**

Salvador Dalí [dah•LEE] (1904–1989) Spain, painter, sculptor. Dalí, a Surrealist, was born in the town of Figueras in the Catalan region of Spain. He had a studio at home when he was growing up. In 1921 he began his studies at the San Fernando Royal Academy of Fine Arts in Madrid. Many of the images in Dalí's work came from dreams. **page 54**

Leonardo da Vinci [dah VIN•chee] (1452–1519) Italy, painter, sculptor. Da Vinci was born in the town of Vinci near Florence, Italy. He was apprenticed to Andrea del Verrocchio, a leading painter and sculptor. In 1478 da Vinci went to work on his own. He was hired to do many paintings, and he became one of the greatest artists of the European Renaissance. **page 18**

Sonia Terk Delaunay [SOHN•yuh terk duh•loh•NAY] (1885–1979) Russia, painter. Delaunay was born in the Ukraine and moved to Paris to work among French painters. In 1964 she became the first living woman to have her work shown at the Louvre [LOOV] Museum. She created abstract images in which colors seemed to move rhythmically. **page 88**

Felix de Weldon (1907–) Austria, sculptor. De Weldon is the only artist in the world to have a monumental sculpture on every continent, including Antarctica. He has created more than 2,000 public works, including 33 in Washington, D.C. De Weldon modeled his *Marine Corps Memorial* sculpture on Joseph Rosenthal's famous photo of U.S. Marines raising the flag on Iwo Jima during World War II. **page 45**

David Diaz United States, illustrator. Diaz, of Rancho La Costa, California, has won many awards, including the highest honor in children's book illustration, the Caldecott Medal. His books include *Neighborhood Odes*, *Smoky Night*, and *Going Home*. **pages 80–81**

James Montgomery Flagg (1877–1960) United States, painter, illustrator. Flagg, born in Pelham Manor, New York, was an American illustrator and poster designer. He worked for several magazines, including *St. Nicholas* and the *Saturday Evening Post*. Flagg also drew caricatures of famous people and painted portraits. **page 48**

Flor Garduño (1957–) Mexico, photographer. Garduño studied at the San Carlos School of Fine Arts in Mexico City. She now travels around Mexico seeking subjects for her photographs and creating a photographic record of Mexico's culture and heritage. **page 94**

Liliana Wilson Grez United States, painter. Grez studied printmaking and painting at Southwest Texas State University from 1990 to 1993. She won first prize in the Ninth Annual Juried Women's Art Exhibit in San Antonio, Texas, and has had her work shown in museums that include the Guadalupe Cultural Arts Center in San Antonio. **page 69**

James Gurney (1958–) United States, author, illustrator. Gurney, the youngest of five children, grew up in Palo Alto, California. He was introduced to dinosaurs when he went to visit a San Francisco museum as a child. By the time he was in high school, Gurney knew he would be an artist. Gurney is both the author and the illustrator of the *Dinotopia* series. **pages 62–63**

Nachum Gutman (1898–1981) Russia, mosaic artist. Gutman was born in Russia and moved to Palestine (Israel) with his family when he was seven. His first one-person show was held at the Bezalel National Museum in Jerusalem in 1933. His work has been shown in museums and galleries around the world. **page 42**

Carol Guzy United States, photographer. Guzy is a photographer for the *Washington Post* newspaper. While studying at the Art Institute of Fort Lauderdale in Florida, she worked as an intern at the *Miami Herald*. Guzy went on to win the Pulitzer Prize for her photography. **page 98**

David Hockney (1937–) England, mixed-media artist. Hockney studied at the Bradford College of Art in England. His first exhibit was in 1963, when he was only twenty-six. In addition to painting, Hockney has designed sets and costumes for operas. He now concentrates on photography. **page 78**

Winslow Homer (1836–1910) United States, painter. Homer was born in Boston, Massachusetts. He was apprenticed to a printer when he was eighteen. When he completed this apprenticeship, he became a freelance illustrator and moved to New York. He traveled widely during his lifetime and painted many different scenes. **page 39**

Edward Hopper (1882–1967) United States, painter. Hopper was an American painter who worked mostly in New York. He made three trips to Europe, but they had little effect on his artistic style. From 1913 until 1923 he stopped painting and began to make a living as a commercial illustrator. When he took up painting again, he became famous for the way he showed his view of life in America. **page 18**

Yusaku Kamekura [yoo•SAH•koo kah•meh•KOO•ruh] (1915–) Japan, graphic designer. Kamekura was born in Japan. He has designed many books, magazines, symbols, and neon signs. His most widely known works in the United States have been the emblem and posters for the 1960 Olympic Games in Tokyo. **page 49**

Jacob Lawrence (1917–) United States, painter. Lawrence was born in Atlantic City, New Jersey. At age fifteen he decided to become a painter. One of his most famous works, *The Migration of the Negro*, includes his parents as models. In 1941 Lawrence became the first African American artist represented in the permanent collection of the Museum of Modern Art. **page 44**

René Magritte [ruh•NAY muh•GREET] (1898–1967) Belgium, painter. Magritte studied at the Academe des Beaux-Arts in Brussels, Belgium, where he was exposed to many art movements, such as Cubism, Futurism, and Symbolism. He found his own unique style and is today among the best known of the Surrealist painters. **page 68**

Stanley Marsh 3 United States, sculptor. Marsh, a Texas millionaire Pop artist, created what he called "the world's largest soft pool table" on a farm outside Amarillo, Texas. Marsh offered a piece of land to a group of artists called the Ant Farm, and it is on this land that Cadillac Ranch is built. **page 71**

Homer Dodge Martin (1836–1897) United States, painter. Martin was born in New York and had a lifelong love of nature. Despite (or perhaps because of) being barely able to see, he studied nature constantly, making mental images of natural scenes and painting them. In his final years, he continued to paint even though he was almost completely blind. **page 28**

Henri Matisse [ahn•REE mah•TEES] (1869–1954) France, painter. Matisse was born in the Picardy region of France. He was the leader of the Fauvist movement in painting. He was active as an artist until the end of his life. When he was too weak to stand at an easel, he created papercuts. Many people consider him to be the most important French painter of the twentieth century. **pages 56, 79**

Florence McClung (1896–1992) United States, painter. McClung lived in Dallas from age three until her death. She was married to Rufus McClung, a cotton broker. She began to study art in 1927 and joined the Taos Society of Artists. McClung liked to paint scenes that could only be found in Texas. Her Texas landscapes brought her national attention. **page 77**

Michelangelo Buonarroti
[bwoh•nar•RAH•tee]
(1475–1564) Italy, painter, sculptor. Michelangelo was born in the small village of Caprese near Arezzo, Italy. His father arranged for him to work and study with the painter Domenico Ghirlandajo when he was just thirteen. By the time he was sixteen years old, Michelangelo had produced at least two relief sculptures. He went on to become one of the greatest artists of the European Renaissance, excelling in painting, sculpture, and architecture. **page 114**

Arthur Mole (1889–1947) United States, photographer. Mole began his career at the age of seventeen when he became the apprentice to a Chicago photographer. Just six months later, Mole started his own photography business. He is best known for his elaborate "living photography" tributes. **page 52**

Piet Mondrian [PEET MOHN•dree•ahn] (1872–1944) Netherlands, painter. Mondrian was born in the Netherlands. Along with several other Dutch artists, he created a style of nonrepresentational art that had a great influence on artists, architects, and designers. In his paintings, Mondrian wanted to show that people can live in harmony with the universe. **page 88**

Michael Naranjo
[nah•RAHN•hoh] (1944–) United States, sculptor. Naranjo was born in Santa Clara Pueblo in New Mexico. He dreamed of being a sculptor but was blinded in an accident in the Vietnam War. Despite being blind, Naranjo decided to sculpt. He uses his memory of things he has seen to create figures out of wax or stone. **page 31**

Louise Nevelson
(1899–1988) Russia, sculptor. Nevelson was born in Kiev, Russia. When she was six years old, her family moved to the United States. From 1929 to 1930 she studied at the Art Students League in New York. She worked as an assistant to artist Diego Rivera and had her first one-person show in 1941. **page 65**

Claes Oldenburg [KLAHS OHL•den•burg] (1929–) Sweden, sculptor. Oldenburg was born in Stockholm, Sweden, but his family moved to the United States when he was seven. He studied at the Art Institute of Chicago. He is married to artist Coosje van Bruggen, and has worked with her on several large-scale public projects. **page 70**

 **Diana Ong** (1940–) United States, multi-media. Ong studied at the National Academy of Art and the School of Visual Arts. Her work has been exhibited and sold in more than thirty countries and displayed on numerous book jackets. Ong works in several media including watercolor, acrylic, ceramic, and computer art. **page 84**

 **John Outterbridge** (1933–) United States, sculptor. Outterbridge is an assemblage artist who was born in South Carolina. He often makes his sculptures out of the rusted steel and iron that his father collected throughout his lifetime. **page 64**

 **Nam June Paik** (1932–) Korea, composer, video artist. Paik studied music and art history at Tokyo University. In the 1960s he was known as an electronic composer and producer of "action concerts." In 1964 he moved to New York and began making video art and TV sculptures. **page 112**

 **I. M. Pei** (1917–) China, architect. Ieoh Ming Pei was born in Canton, China. He studied at Harvard University and later became an assistant professor at Harvard Graduate School of Design. His works include the Dallas City Hall building, the National Gallery of Art East building, and the Rock 'n' Roll Hall of Fame and Museum. **page 110**

 **Pablo Picasso** (1881–1973) Spain, painter. Picasso was born in Málaga, Spain, and educated in Paris. He was one of the leaders of the twentieth-century art world. His works changed the way people thought about art. Picasso helped start a style of painting called Cubism. He was greatly influenced by African sculpture when he began painting in the Cubist style. **page 92**

 **Jerry Pinkney** (1939–) United States, illustrator. Pinkney grew up in Philadelphia, Pennsylvania, and graduated from the Philadelphia Museum College of Art. His career began in commercial illustration— designing ads and greeting cards. His first book was a collection of West African folktales. Since then, he has won some of the highest awards in children's illustration. **page 12**

 **Horace Pippin** (1888–1946) United States, painter. Pippin left school at the age of fourteen to work on a farm. He had no formal art training, but he began painting seriously after his right arm was partially paralyzed as a result of an injury in World War I. Many of his works show scenes from the Bible or from the daily life of African American families. **page 82**

Frederic Remington (1861–1909) United States, painter, sculptor. Remington was born in his grand-mother's house in New York. During his career he produced over three thousand illustrations and paintings and twenty-two sculptures. Remington's work depicts the settling of the West. **page 14**

Betsy Graves Reyneau [ray•NOH] (1888–1964) United States, painter. Reyneau was born in Battle Creek, Michigan. She studied art all over the world including Boston, Paris, and Rome. Some of her portraits were featured in a national exhibition, and two of her works hang in the National Portrait Gallery in Washington, D.C. **page 36**

Bridget Riley (1931–) England, painter. Riley was born in London, England. She studied at Goldsmiths College of Art and at the Royal College of Art. She has traveled widely but continues to live and work in London. **page 58**

Diego Rivera (1886–1957) Mexico, painter. Rivera, a Mexican artist, is famous for his huge murals. Rivera was only ten years old when he began taking art courses at the Academy of San Carlos in Mexico City. He once said, "In my work, I tell the story of my nation, Mexico—its history, its Revolution, its amazing Indian past, and its present-day popular traditions." **pages 116–117**

Miriam Schapiro (1923–) Canada, painter. When Schapiro created *Heartland*, she drew on the tradition of American quilting. Much of her work is inspired by the talents of women, who for hundreds of years have expressed artistic abilities in the form of household crafts such as quilting, embroidering, and sewing. **page 125**

Jane Wooster Scott United States, painter. Scott was born in the small town of Havertown, Pennsylvania. She attended just one semester of college before moving to New York to work in television and movies. After she retired from acting, she began painting as a hobby. She began her professional painting career in 1973. **page 38**

George Segal (1924–) United States, sculptor, painter. Segal was operating a chicken farm when he first began painting. He started to experiment with sculpture in 1958, using wire netting. He has produced several public sculptures, including *The Rush Hour* in London. **page 103**

Gilbert Stuart (1755–1828) United States, painter. Stuart was born in Rhode Island before the United States became a nation. He painted several of our earliest Presidents. Stuart also created a very famous engraving—the relief portrait of George Washington that appears on the one-dollar bill. **page 36**

Robert Summers
(1940–) United States, sculptor. Summers was born and raised in Glen Rose, Texas, and has created many sculptures throughout Texas and the United States. Summers is especially interested in depicting the lore of the West, which he enjoyed as a boy and has studied seriously as an adult. **page 32**

Wayne Thiebaud
[TEE•boh] (1920–) United States, painter. Thiebaud was born in Mesa, Arizona, and held various art-related jobs in New York and California. He is best known for his texture paintings of ice cream, cakes, and hot dogs. **page 51**

Alma Woodsey Thomas
(1891–1978) United States, educator, painter. Thomas was born in Columbus, Georgia. In 1924 she began teaching art at a junior high school. It was not until after she had retired from teaching that she had time to devote to painting. **page 89**

Coosje van Bruggen
[KOOS•yeh van BROO•gen] (1942–) Netherlands, sculptor. Van Bruggen was born in Groningen in the Netherlands and earned a degree in art history from the University of Groningen. She began to work with Claes Oldenburg on such projects as *Trowel I* in 1976. She married Oldenburg in 1977. **page 70**

Vincent van Gogh
[van GOH] (1853–1890) Netherlands, painter. Van Gogh was born in Zundert, Netherlands. He created about 800 paintings and drawings in only ten years, during which he suffered from severe mental illness. Next to Rembrandt, he is generally considered the greatest Dutch painter. **pages 24, 90**

Pablita Velarde (Hardin)
[pab•LEET•uh vel•AHR•day] (1918–) United States, painter. Velarde, a Tewa artist, was born in Santa Clara Pueblo, New Mexico. She broke away from tradition by deciding to become a painter, a career that only men were expected to choose. Her paintings show the traditions of her people. She is also the author of a book of Tewa legends. **page 122**

Andy Warhol (1928–1987) United States, painter. Warhol was born in McKeesport, Pennsylvania. He studied at the Carnegie Technical College and then worked as a commercial illustrator and store window designer in New York. He was one of the leaders of the Pop Art movement. **page 50**

Anna Belle Lee Washington
United States, painter. Washington, the oldest of seven children, grew up in Detroit, Michigan. Her first job was as a social services clerk. Many years later, she moved to St. Simons Island, Georgia, to retire. Instead she began a new career, starting by taking drawing and painting lessons at the Coastal Center for the Arts there. **page 23**

Leah Ann Washington
United States, photographer. Washington was born in New Orleans, Louisiana, where her mother owned and operated a photographic studio. She attended Brooks Institute of Photography and became the school's first African American woman graduate. Both of her brothers are photographers as well. **page 99**

Frank Lloyd Wright
(1867–1959) United States, architect. Wright was born in Wisconsin and created buildings all over the world. He attended the University of Wisconsin. Some of his most famous works include the Guggenheim Museum in New York and the Madison Convention Center in Wisconsin. **page 111**

Andrew Wyeth (1917–)
United States, painter. Andrew is the son of N. C. Wyeth, a famous illustrator. Like his father, Andrew developed a love of nature, a sense of romance, and great artistic ability. His work is a combination of abstract style and realistic detail. **page 74**

Lance Wyman (1937–)
United States, designer. Wyman was born in Newark, New Jersey. He studied design at the Pratt Institute in Brooklyn, New York. His works include the first postage stamp honoring Dr. Martin Luther King, Jr.; maps for the Washington, D.C., Metro train system; and posters for the World Cup of Soccer, held at Mexico City in 1971. **page 49**

GLOSSARY

The Glossary contains important art terms and their definitions. Each word is respelled as it would be in a dictionary. When you see this mark (´) after a syllable, pronounce that syllable with more force than the other syllables.

add, **ā**ce, c**â**re, p**ä**lm; **e**nd, **ē**qual; **i**t, **ī**ce; **o**dd, **ō**pen, **ô**rder; t**ŏŏ**k, p**ōō**l; **u**p, b**û**rn; y**ōō** as *u* in *fuse*; **oi**l; p**ou**t; ə as *a* in *above, e* in *sicken, i* in *possible, o* in *melon, u* in *circus*; **ch**eck; ri**ng**; **th**in; ~~**th**~~is; **zh** as in *vision*

abstract [ab´strakt] A style of art that does not show a scene in a realistic way. Abstract art uses the elements and principles of design to convey ideas and feelings.

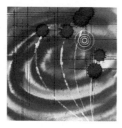

abstract

advance [ad•vans´] To move forward—speaking of a background color that seems to jump outward. (*See also* recede.)

analogous colors [ə•na´lə•gəs kəl´ərz] Colors that are closely related and near each other on the color wheel. Families of analogous colors include the warm colors (reds, oranges, and yellows) and the cool colors (greens, blues, and violets). (*See also* cool colors, warm colors.)

animation [a•nə•mā´shən] The art of making objects, such as drawings of cartoon characters, appear to move; making a motion picture using still drawings or objects. (*See also* frame.)

arbitrary colors [är´bə•trer•ē kəl´ərz] Colors that go beyond what is natural or common in a scene.

arch [ärch] A curved structure over an opening such as a door or window.

assemblage [ə•sem´blij] A piece of art made by combining a collection of three-dimensional objects.

asymmetry, asymmetrical [ā•si´mə•trē, ā•sə•me´tri•kəl] Having a kind of balance in which things on each side of a center line are different, but still look balanced. (*See also* balance, symmetry.)

atmospheric perspective [at•mə•sfir´ik pər•spek´tiv] The illusion of depth and distance created by using dull, pale colors and hazy details in the background of a painting. (*See also* perspective.)

background [bak´ground] The part of a work of art that appears to be in the back, farthest away from the viewer. (*See also* foreground, middle ground.)

balance [ba´ləns] The arrangement of elements in a work of art; how important the elements in one part are compared to those in other parts. (*See also* asymmetry, symmetry.)

brushstroke [brush´strōk] The application of paint with a paintbrush. Also, the look of paint that has been applied with a paintbrush.

center of interest [sen´tər əv in´trest] The most important area in a work of art. All other parts should center around, provide background for, or draw attention to this area.

cityscape [si´tē•skāp] A painting or drawing showing a view of a city.

cityscape

collage [kə•läzh´] A work of art created by gluing bits of paper, fabric, scraps, photographs, or other materials to a flat surface.

collage

color [kəl´ər] The visual sensation produced when different wavelengths of light strike the eye.

complementary colors [kom•plə•men´tə•rē kəl´ərz] Colors that are opposite on the color wheel and that contrast with each other. Pairs of complementary colors include orange/blue and violet/yellow.

composition [kom•pə•zi´shən] The arrangement or design of elements in an artwork.

contrast [kon´trast] A notable difference between two things; for example, light and shadow. (*See also* complementary colors.)

cool colors [kōol kəl´ərz] The family of related colors ranging from the greens through the violets. (*See also* analogous colors, warm colors.)

cross-hatching [krôs´ha•ching] Shading done by drawing closely set parallel lines that cross one another.

daguerreotype [də•ge´rō•tīp] An early form of photography.

depth [depth] The apparent distance from front to back or from near to far in an artwork.

detail [di•tāl´] A small, often less important feature of a person or an object.

diagonal [dī•a´gə•nəl] Slanting between horizontal and vertical. (*See also* line.)

diorama [dī•ə•ra´mə] A scene, usually smaller than in real life, in which three-dimensional models are displayed against a realistic painted background.

diorama

emphasis [em´fə•sis] The drawing of attention to important areas or objects in a work of art.

Expressionists [ik•spre´shə•nists] Artists who used a style of art that stresses emotion over realism in proportion, color, and so on.

expressive [ik•spre´siv] Showing feelings or ideas.

flip book [flip book] A simple form of animation in which pages of drawings are flipped through by hand to create the illusion of movement. (*See also* animation.)

flip book

focus [fō´kəs] The clearest possible image seen through a camera lens.

folk artists [fōk ärt´ists] People who create traditional art using styles and techniques that have been handed down through generations.

foreground [fôr´ground] The part of a work of art that appears to be in the front, nearest to the viewer. (*See also* background, middle ground.)

foreshortened [fôr•shôr´tənd] Drawn or painted in a way that shows length or depth. For example, to make an object that is pointing at the viewer seem lifelike, the artist shortens its length. (*See also* perspective.)

form [fôrm] A three-dimensional unit in an artwork, such as a cube.

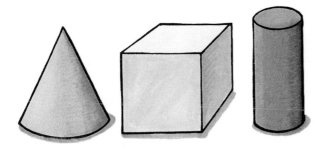

form

frame [frām] A border that encloses an artwork. Also, one of a set of many still pictures, each slightly different, created for an animated cartoon or movie.

geometric [jē•ə•me´trik] Based on simple shapes such as rectangles, triangles, circles, straight lines, or sharp, angled designs.

harmony [här´mə•nē] An orderly, pleasing state, such as when colors or objects blend well together in an artwork.

hatching [ha´ching] Shading done by drawing tiny, closely set parallel lines.

highlighting [hī´lī•ting] Using color to draw attention to or to emphasize.

horizon [hə•rī´zən] A level line where water or land seems to end and the sky begins.

horizon

horizontal symmetry [hôr´ə•zon•təl si´mə•trē] A condition in which the top and the bottom of a picture or object are alike.

illuminated pages [i•loo´mə•nā•təd pāj´əz] Pages having fancy designs and pictures, often decorated with gold or silver to make them look as if they are lit up.

illusions [i•loo´zhənz] False impressions, such as those brought about by artistic techniques or by nature.

impasto [im•pas´tō] A technique in which thick paint is applied in layers, creating a heavily textured appearance.

Impressionists [im•pre´shə•nists] Artists of the late 1800s and early 1900s who showed nature in new ways. They often used dots and strokes of bright colors in their paintings. Many Impressionists concentrated on showing the effects of light on people and objects.

incising [in•sī´zing] Cutting or carving a design into clay objects.

incising

intermediate colors [in•tər•mē´dē•ət kəl´ərz] A color created by mixing a primary color with a secondary color. Sometimes called a tertiary color. (*See also* primary colors, secondary colors.)

landscape [land´skāp] A painting or drawing showing a view of a natural scene, such as mountains, rivers, flowers, fields, or forests.

line [līn] A slender, continuous mark moving through space that can vary in length, width, direction, shape, and color.

linear perspective [li´nē•ər pər•spek´tiv] The use of converging lines to show depth and distance in a picture. Lines that are parallel in nature, such as railroad tracks, come together at the vanishing point in a picture. (*See also* perspective.)

material [mə•tir´ē•əl] Basic substance from which other things are made. Clay, plaster of Paris, and wood are examples of art materials.

middle ground [mi´dəl ground] The part of a work of art that lies between the foreground and the background. (*See also* foreground, background.)

minarets [mi•nə•retz´] Slender towers with one or more balconies, attached to a mosque.

minarets

mixed-media [mikst•mē´dē•ə] A term used to describe an artwork that uses two or more media, such as painting and collage.

mobile [mō´bēl] A type of sculpture in which objects are suspended and balanced so that they move with currents of air.

mood [mood] An overall feeling or emotion.

mosaics [mō•zā´iks] Artworks made by fitting small pieces of colored paper, glass, tile, stone, or other similar materials, called *tesserae*, onto a background.

movement [moov´mənt] The arrangement of elements in an artwork to create a sense of motion.

mural [myoor´əl] A very large painting done on a wall.

mural

negative space [ne´gə•tiv spās] The empty space surrounding shapes or forms in a work of art. (*See also* positive space, space.)

nonrepresentational [non•re•pri•zen•tā´shə•nəl] A style of art that does not show recognizable objects.

Op Art [op ärt] An abstract style of art, based on visual illusions, that was popular in the 1960s.

optical illusion [op´ti•kəl i•loo´zhən] A vision, human-made or natural, that tricks the eye and the brain.

organic [ôr•ga´nik] Having a quality that resembles living things. Also, having a flowing, rounded shape.

ornamentation [ôr•nə•men•tā´shən] The use of details or items such as jewelry to create a beautiful appearance.

overlapping [ō´vər•lap•ing] A technique in which one shape in a painting covers up some part of another. Since partly covered objects appear to be farther away, this technique is used to show distance.

papier-mâché [pā•pər•mə•shā´] An art material made of paper torn into strips or made into pulp and mixed with paste.

pattern [pa´tərn] The repetition of shapes, lines, or colors in a design.

perspective [pər•spek´tiv] The art of drawing three-dimensional objects on a two-dimensional surface. Perspective is achieved by creating the illusion of depth and distance. Two types of perspective are *atmospheric* and *linear*.

photogram [fō´tə•gram] A technique for producing an image by placing an object on light-sensitive paper and exposing the paper to light. Sometimes called a sun print.

photomontage [fō•tə•mon•täzh´] Photographs that are arranged into one picture expressing a single theme.

photomontage

Pop Art [pop ärt] A style of art—based on popular foods, fads, and brand names—made famous in New York in the 1950s.

porcelain [pôr´sə•lən] A fine-grained, hard type of clay used to make dishes, vases, and small statues.

portrait [pôr´trət] A painting, photograph, or other work of art showing a person. Portraits usually show only the face but can include part or all of the body as well.

portrait

pose [pōz] The position of a subject for a portrait or photograph. (*See also* portrait.)

positive space [pä´zə•tiv spās] The solid shape of an object in a work of art. (*See also* negative space, space.)

primary colors [prī´mer•ē kəl´ərz] The colors—red, yellow, and blue—that in different combinations produce all other colors except white. (*See also* intermediate colors, secondary colors.)

proportions [prə•pôr´shənz] The relationships of placement and size among objects in a composition.

quilts [kwilts] Bedcovers made by sewing scraps of cloth together.

recede [ri•sēd′] To move backward—speaking of foreground colors that seem to move back. (*See also* advance.)

relative size [re′lə•tiv sīz] The size of an object when compared to the objects around it.

rhythm [ri′t͟həm] The regular repetition of lines, shapes, colors, or patterns in a work of art.

scale [skāl] The size of an object in an artwork compared to its original size. If a picture is drawn *to scale*, all of its parts are equally smaller or larger than the original.

score [skôr] To mark by scratching or cutting.

sculpture [skulp′chər] A carving, model, or other three-dimensional piece of art.

secondary colors [se′kən•der•ē kəl′ərz] The colors—orange, green, and violet—created by combining two of the three primary colors. Orange is a mixture of red and yellow. Green is a mixture of blue and yellow. Violet is a mixture of red and blue. (*See also* intermediate colors, primary colors.)

shades [shādz] Darker variations of a color made by mixing black with the color. For example, black added to red makes a darker *shade* of red. (*See also* tints.)

shape [shāp] A two-dimensional unit in an artwork, such as a square.

sketch [skech] A simple, quick drawing done to catch the chief features and a general impression of an object or a scene.

sketch

slab method [slab me′thəd] A method of making pottery in which a thick, flat plate or slice of clay is cut into shapes that are then joined together to form an object.

slip [slip] A creamy mixture of clay and water or vinegar used to cement together two pieces of clay, such as a handle on a cup.

space [spās] The distance, area, or depth shown in a work of art. Also, the open areas between or inside shapes.

spires [spīrz] Pointed tops of towers or church steeples.

spires

statues [sta´chōōz] Free-standing carved, modeled, or sculpted three-dimensional figures, especially of a person or an animal.

storytelling [stôr´ē•tel•ing] The technique of adding a narrative to a work of art such as a mural or a quilt.

Surrealism [sə•rē´ə•li•zəm] An art movement, beginning in the 1920s, that emphasized images from the unconscious mind, such as from dreams. Surrealists mixed and matched real objects in unusual or impossible combinations, but painted objects in a realistic way.

symbols [sim´bəlz] Things that stand for other things, such as a dove that represents peace.

symmetry, symmetrical [si´mə•trē, sə•me´tri•kəl] Having a kind of balance in which things on each side of a center line or around a central point appear the same. (*See also* asymmetry, balance.)

synthetic [sin•the´tik] A human-made material. Something that is not created naturally, such as plastic and steel.

tempera [tem´pə•rə] Water-soluble paint that does not allow light to pass through. Also called poster paint.

tesserae [te´sə•rē] The individual pieces used to make a mosaic. (*See also* mosaics.)

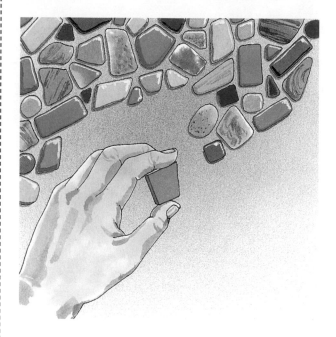

tesserae

texture [teks´chər] The way a surface looks or feels—rough, smooth, silky, shiny, or dull.

theme [thēm] The subject or main idea in an artistic work.

three-dimensional [thrē•də•men´shə•nəl] Having length, width, and depth. A sculpture is three-dimensional, but a drawing is two-dimensional. (*See also* two-dimensional.)

tints [tints] Lighter variations of a color made by adding white to the color. For example, white added to blue makes a lighter blue *tint*. (*See also* shades.)

trompe l'oeil [trômp•loi´] An image that appears to be real rather than painted. *Trompe l'oeil* is French for "tricks the eye."

two-dimensional [to͞o•də•men´shə•nəl] Having length and width, but not depth; flat. Paintings and drawings are examples of two-dimensional art forms. (*See also* three-dimensional.)

type [tīp] A style of printing.

unity [yo͞o´nə•tē] A quality of oneness, or a pleasing sense, achieved by connecting all the different elements in an artwork.

value [val´yo͞o] The lightness or darkness of colors. For example, white and yellow have a light value; black and purple have a dark value.

vanishing point [va´ni•shing point] In linear perspective, the place on the horizon where parallel lines appear to meet or converge. The part of the art that looks farthest away. (*See also* perspective.)

variety [və•rī´ə•tē] An assortment of lines, colors, forms, shapes, textures, or other elements in a work of art.

vertical symmetry [vər´ti•kəl si´mə•trē] A condition in which the left and right sides of a picture or an object are matched.

warm colors [wärm kəl´ərz] The family of related colors ranging from the reds through the browns. (*See also* analogous colors, cool colors.)

watercolor [wô´tər•kəl•ər] A transparent paint made by mixing powdered colors with a binding material, such as glue, and water. The term also refers to a painting done with watercolors.

weaving [wē´ving] The process of turning thread or yarn into cloth. Artwork created by lacing together fibers—such as threads or yarn—on a loom.

weaving

ARTISTS & ARTWORKS

ACKNOWLEDGMENTS

PHOTO CREDITS

Cover
Superstock

Table of Contents:
Harcourt Brace & Company
6, Weronica Ankarorn; 7, Weronica Ankarorn.

Other
5(l), Steve Helbert/AP/Wide World Photos; 5(r), Corbis-Bettmann; 8(l), Michael Holford; 8(r), Reunion des Musees Nationaux; 9, Scala/Art Resource, NY.

Front Matter:
11,Richard Nowitz; 12-13, From In for Winter, Out for Spring by Arnold Adoff, illustrated by Jerry Pinkney. Harcourt Brace & Company. Sketch courtesy of Jerry Pinkney;

Unit 1:
Harcourt Brace & Company
17(c)&(b),Weronica Ankarorn; 19(b), Weronica Ankarorn; 23(c)&(b), Weronica Ankarorn; 25(t)&(b), Weronica Ankarorn; 29(ct&b)(b), Weronica Ankarorn; 31(ct&b)(b), Weronica Ankarorn; 33, Weronica Ankarorn.

Other
14, Frederic S. Remington, The Fall of the Cowboy, 1895, oil on canvas, 1961.230. Copyright Amon Carter Museum, Fort Worth, Texas; 16, Giraudon/Art Resource, NY; 17(t), Catalogue No. 234314, Department of Anthropology, Smithsonian Institution; 18(t), The Royal Collection (c) Her Majesty Queen Elizabeth II; 18(b), The Metropolitan Museum of Art, Hugo Kastor Fund, 1962. (62.95); 20, Courtesy, Barbara Bash; 21, From Tree of Life: The World of the African Baobab by Barbara Bash. Little, Brown & Company; 22, The Metropolitan Museum of Art, Gift of Mrs. Russell Sage, 1908. (08.228); 23(t), Superstock; 24, Christie's Images/ Superstock; 26, courtesy, Bob Phillips; 27(all), courtesy, Bob Phillips; 28(t) The Armand Hammer Collection, UCLA at the Armand Hammer Museum of Art and Cultural Center, Los Angeles, CA; 28(b), The Metropolitan Museum of Art, Gift of Several Gentlemen, 1897. (97,32); 29(t), Courtesy, Ping Wang; 30 Photo Galerie Maeght, Paris; 31(t), Mark Nohl; 32, Jeff Shaw/Mercury Pictures.

Unit 2:
Harcourt Brace & Company
37(all), Weronica Ankarorn; 40, Weronica Ankarorn; 41(both), Weronica Ankarorn; 45(b), Weronica Ankarorn; 49(b), Weronica Ankarorn; 51(b), Weronica Ankarorn; 53, Weronica Ankarorn.

Other
34, Wide World Photos; 35, FDR Library; 36(l), White House Historical Association; 36(r), National Portrait Gallery, Gift of the Harmon Foundation, Smithsonian Institution/Art Resource, NY; 38, Collection of Mr. and Mrs. Ernest Borgnine/Superstock; 39, The Saint Louis Art Museum; 42, Eddie Gerald/Documentary Photography; 43, Scala/Art Resource,NY; 44(l), Robert Rathe/Folio; 44(r), Jacob Lawrence, "The Migrants Arrived in Great Numbers" Panel 40 from the Migration Series. Photograph © 1998 The Museum of Modern Art, New York; 45(t), Peter Gridley/FPG; 46, Philip & Karen Smith/Tony Stone Images; 47(l), Chris Kleponis/Woodfin Camp & Associates; 47(r), Steve Helbert/AP/Wide World Photos; 48, Corbis-Bettmann; 49(tl), ©IOC/Olympic Museum Collection; 49(tr), ©IOC/Olympic Museum Collections; 50, Staadsgalerie, Stuttgart; 51(t), Wayne Thiebaud; 52, Mole & Thomas photograph, negative #ICHi-16299/Chicago Historical Society.

Unit 3:
Harcourt Brace & Company
57(all), Weronica Ankarorn; 63(b), Weronica Ankarorn; 65(b), Weronica Ankarorn;
71(c)&(b), Weronica Ankarorn.

Other
54, photo © DESCHARNES & DESCHARNES; 55, UPI/Corbis-Bettmann; 56, The Museum of Modern Art, New York. The Louis E. Stern Collection. Photograph © 1998 The Museum of Modern Art, New York; 58, Collection Walker Art Center, Minneapolis. Gift of Mr. and Mrs. Julius E. Davis, 1981; 59, Archer M. Huntington Art Gallery, The University of Texas at Austin, Gift of Mari and James A. Michener, 1991. Photo by George Holmes. © 1988 Richard Anuszkiewicz/Licensed by VAGA, New York, NY; 60, Philadelphia Museum of Art, George W. Elkins Collection; 61, Travelpix/FPG International; 62-63, ©1998 James Gurney. All Rights Reserved. Published by Arrangement with Turner Publishing, Inc.; 64, California Afro-American Museum Foundation; 65(t),

Museum Ludwig © Rheinisches Bildarchiv, Museen der Stadt Köln; 66(both), Courtesy of Lily Yeh; 67, Courtesy of Lily Yeh; 68, Hersovici/Art Resource, NY; 69, Courtesy, Women & Their Work, Austin, Texas; 70, Collection Walker Art Center, Minneapolis, Gift of Frederick R. Weisman in honor of his parents, William & Mary Weisman; 71, McSpadden Photography; 72, Al Messerschmidt/Folio.

Unit 4:
Harcourt Brace & Company
77(c)(b), Weronica Ankarorn; 83(b), Weronica Ankarorn; 85, Weronica Ankarorn; 89(c)&(b), Weronica Ankarorn; 91, Weronica Ankarorn.

Other
74, Faraway, drybrush,1952, Copyright 1997 Andrew Wyeth. Photograph Courtesy of Wyeth Collection; 75, Richard Schulman/Gamma Liaison; 76, Trail Riders, Gift of the Artist © 1998 Board of Trustees, National Gallery Of Art, Washington. 1975.42.1(2678)/PA. © 1998Thomas H. Benton & Rita P. Benton Testamentary Trusts/Licensed by VAGA, New York, NY; 77(t), Dallas Museum of Art, gift of Florence E. McClung; 78, David Hockney, "Nichols Canyon", 1980, acrylic, 84" X 60". © David Hockney; 79, The Louis E. Stern Collection, The Museum of Modern Art. Photograph ©1998 The Museum of Modern Art, New York; 80(t), Cecelia Diaz Zieba; 80(b), David Diaz; 81(t) & (b), David Diaz; 82, The Metropolitan Museum of Art, Arthur Hoppock Hearn Fund, 1958. (58.26); 83(t), Untitled, 1976, National Gallery of Art, Washington, Gift of the Collectors Committee. 1977.76.1.(SC) A-17994. Photo by Philip A. Charles.; 84, Superstock; 86, AP/Wide World Photos; 87, AP/Wide World Photos; 88(t), Piet Mondrian, "Broadway Boogie Woogie". 1942-43. Oil on canvas, 50 x 50" (127x127 cm) The Museum of Modern Art, New York. Given anonymously. Photograph © 1998 The Museum of Modern Art, New York; 88(b), Christie's Images/Superstock; 89(t)National Museum of American Art, Washington, D C /Art Resource,New York, 90, Vincent van Gogh. The Starry Night.(1989). Oil on canvas, 29x36 1/4" (73.3 x 92.1 cm). The Museum of Modern Art, New York. Acquired through the Lillie P. Bliss Request. Photograph ©1998 The Museum of Modern Art.; 92, Pablo Picasso, Three Musicians, Fontainebleau, summer, 1921, oil on canvas, 6'7" x 7' 3 3/4". The Museum of Modern Art, New York. Mrs. Simon Guggenheim Fund. Photograph © 1998 The Museum of Modern Art, New York.

Unit 5:
Harcourt Brace & Company
99(c)&(b), Weronica Ankarorn; 103(c)&(b), Weronica Ankarorn; 105(ct&b)(b), Weronica Ankarorn; 109(c)&(b), Weronica Ankarorn; 111 (c)&(b), Weronica Ankarorn.

Other
94, Flor Garduño; 95, Vilma Slomp; 96(l), Bridgman/Art Resource,NY; 96(r), Moshe Caine/The Israel Museum, Jerusalem; 97, Freer Gallery of Art, Smithsonian Institution;98, 1994 Washington Post Photo by Carol Guzy. Reprinted with permission; 99(t), Leah A. Washington; 100, Marina Ancona; 101, George Ancona; 102(l), Michael Holford; 102, (r)Reunion des Musees Nationaux; 103(t), Sidney Janis Gallery ©1998 George Segal/Licensed by VAGA, New York, NY; 104, Motion Picture & TV Photo Archive; 105 (t), Motion Picture & TV Photo Archive; 106, Courtesy of Karen Kiser; 107(t), Motion Picture & TV Photo Archive; 107(b), Courtesy of Karen Kiser; 108, Luiz C. Marigo/Peter Arnold, Inc.; 109 (t), The Granger Collection, New York; 110, Stephen Johnson/ Tony Stone Images; 111(t), Bernard Boutrit/Woodfin Camp & Associates; 112, Courtesy of the artist and Holly Solomon Gallery, New York.

Unit 6:
Harcourt Brace & Company
119(ct&b)(b), Weronica Ankarorn; 123(c)&(b), Weronica Ankarorn; 125(c)&(b), Weronica Ankarorn; 129(c)&(b), Weronica Ankarorn; 131(c)&(b), Weronica Ankarorn; 133, Weronica Ankarorn.

Other
114, The Granger Collection, New York; 115, Scala/Art Resource, NY; 116-117, Photograph © 1997 The Detroit Institute of Arts, Gift of Edsel B. Ford; 118(l), National Museum of Ireland; 118(r), Ann Ronan Picture Library; 119(t), Spode Museum Trust; 120, Carollee Pelos, from Spectacular Vernacular; N.Y.:Aperture, 1996; 121, Carollee Pelos, from Spectacular Vernacular; N.Y.:Aperture, 1996; 122, Denver Art Museum collection; 123(t), Photograph © 1997 The Detroit Institute of the Arts Founders Society Purchase # 81.425; 124, The Metropolitan Museum of Art, Bequest of Margaret Brown Potvin, 1987. (1988.134); 125(t), Gift of the Women for Special Acquisitions and Council of 101/Orlando Museum of Art; 126, Kelly Culpepper; 127(both), Kelly Culpepper;

128(t), The Metropolitan Museum of Art, Dodge Fund, 1933. (33.35.3); 128(b), Courtesy of the Trustees of the Victoria & Albert Museum; 129 (t), JJ Foxx/NYC; 130, K. Kitamura; 131, Planet Art; 132, Bob Daemmrich Photography.

Art Safety:
134- 135 Harcourt Brace and Company/Terry Sinclair.

Exploring Art Techniques:
138(t), Susan McCartney/Photo Researchers; 140-151, Weronica Ankarorn/Harcourt Brace & Company.

Elements and Principles:
152-153 (t), Damien Lovegrove/SPL/Photo Researchers;152 (bl), Paul McCormick/The Image Bank; 152 (bc), Peggy & Ronald Barnett/The Stock Market; 152 (br), Gabe Palmer/The Stock Market; 153 (t), Harald Sund/The Image Bank; 153 (cl), Will & Deni McIntyre/Photo Researchers; 153 (cr), Jim Corwin/Photo Researchers; 153 (bl), John Gillmoure/The Stock Market; 153 (br), F. Tetefolle/Explorer/Photo Researchers; 154 (tl), Renee Lynn/Photo Researchers; 154 (tr), Nuridsany et Perennou/Photo Researchers; 154 (cl), Alan Carruthers/Photo Researchers; 154 (cr), Frank P. Rossotto/The Stock Market; 154 (bl), Grafton Marshall Smith/The Stock Market; 154 (br), Tom Bean/The Stock Market; 155 (tl), Stephen Marks/The Image Bank; 155 (tc), Charles D. Winters/Photo Researchers; 155 (tr), Lee F. Snyder/Photo Researchers; 155 (c), Doug Plummer/Photo Researchers; 155 (bl), Phil Jude/SPL/Photo Researchers; 155 (br), James Carmichael/The Image Bank; 156 (tl), Ed Bock/The Stock Market; 156 (tc), David Parker/SPL/Photo Researchers; 156 (cl), Adrienne Hart-Davis/SPL/Photo Researchers; 156 (cr), Chromosohm/Sohm/Photo Researchers; 156 (br), Murray Alcosser/The Image Bank; 157 (tc), Arthur Beck/The Stock Market; 157 (tr), Raga/The Stock Market; 157 (c), Chris Collins/The Stock Market; 157 (bl), B. Seitz/Photo Researchers; 157 (br), Zefa Germany/The Stock Market; 158 (tl), Michael Lustbader/Photo Researchers; 158 (tr), Alan & Linda Detrick/Photo Researchers; 158 (c), Brownie Harris/The Stock Market; 158 (cl), Bryan F. Peterson/The Stock Market ; 159 (tl), Stuart Dee/The Image Bank; 159 (tcl), Wm. Whitehurst/The Stock Market; 159 (tr), Patricio Robles Gil/Bruce Coleman, Inc.; 159 (bl), Sonya Jacobs/The Stock Market; 159 (bc), Bob Abraham/The Stock Market; 159 (br), David Sailors/The Stock Market; 160 (tl), Farley Lewis/Photo Researchers; 160 (tr), P. Saloutos/The Stock Market; 160 (cl), Art Wolfe/Tony Stone Images; 160 (c), Michal Heron/The Stock Market; 160 (cr), Dan McCoy/The Stock Market; 160 (b), Aaron Rezny/The Stock Market; 160 (bc), Jeff Hunter/The Image Bank; 161 (tl), Zefa Germany/The Stock Market; 161 (tr), Bryan Peterson/The Stock Market; 161 (c), Charles Krebs/The Stock Market; 161 (bl), Viviane Moos/The Stock Market; 161 (br), Jack Baker/The Image Bank; 162 (tl), Zefa Germany/The Stock Market; 162 (tr), Richard J. Green/Photo Researchers; 162 (c), Art Stein/Photo Researchers; 162 (bl), Dr. Jeremy Burgess/SPL/Photo Researchers; 162 (br), Joseph Nettis/Photo Researchers; 163 (t), Kevin Horan/Tony Stone Images; 163 (c), Geoff Dore/Tony Stone Images; 163 (bl), David Hall/Photo Researchers; 163 (br), Jeff Spielman/The Image Bank; 163 (bc), David Sailors/The Stock Market; 164 (tl), Zefa Germany/The Stock Market; 164 (c), Zefa Germany/The Stock Market; 164 (bl), Johnny Johnson/Animals Animals; 164 (br), Anup & Manoj Shah/Animals Animals; 165 (t), Kjell B. Sandved/Photo Researchers; 165 (tl), Will & Deni McIntyre/Photo Researchers; 165 (tr), Mickey Gibson/Animals Animals; 165 (bl), Russell D. Curtis/Photo Researchers; 165 (bc), Grafton Marshall Smith/The Stock Market.

Gallery of Artists (pg. 166-175) by artist's last name:
Anuszkiewicz, Arnold Newman; Bartholdi, Culver Pictures, Inc.; Benton, Corbis-Bettmann; Burke, FDR Library; Calder, Inge Morath/Magnum Photos; Christo, Arnold Newman; Cole, National Portrait Gallery, Smithsonian Institution/Art Resource, NY; DaVinci, Art Resource, NY; Degas, National Portrait Gallery, Smithsonian Institution/Art Resource, NY; Diaz, Cecelia Diaz Zieba; Flagg, Corbis-Bettmann; Garduño, Vilma Stomp; Gaudi, The Granger Collection; Grez, Liliana Wilson Grez; Gurney, Mark Ferri; Guzy, Carol Guzy; Hockney, Woodfin Camp & Associates; Homer, Corbis-Bettmann; Hopper, Pach/Corbis-Bettmann; Lawrence, Eden Arts; Lee, The Glynn Art Association; Magritte, Giraudon/Art Resource, NY; Marsh, Courtesy of Stanley Marsh 3; Martin, The Granger Collection, New York; Matisse, Cartier-Bresson/Magnum Photos; McClung, courtesy Florence McClung; Michelangelo, Superstock; Mole, Chicago Historical Society, ICHi-18716, photographer unknown; Mondrian, Arnold Newman; Naranjo, Mark Nohl; Nevelson, Charles Moore/Black Star; Oldenberg, Charles Moore/Black Star; Ong, Superstock; Outterbridge, California Afro-American Museum Foundation, Willie Robert Middlebrook; Paik, Novovitch/Liaison; Pei, Corbis-Bettmann; Picasso, Giraudon/Art Resource, NY; Pinkney, Alan Orling/Black Star; Pippin, Albright-Knox Art Gallery Buffalo, New York; Riley, Arnold Newman; Rivera, UPI/Corbis-Bettmann; Scott, Scott Art Graphics; Segal, Barbara Pfeffer; Stuart, National Portrait Gallery, Smithsonian Institution/Art Resource, NY; Summer, Ron Kunzman; Thomas, National Museum of American Art, Washington DC, Art Resource, NY; van Bruggen, Thomas Hoepker/Magnum Photos; van Gogh, Erich Lessing/Art Resource; Velarde, US Department of the Interior, Indian Arts and Crafts Board; Warhol, Bernard Gotfryd/Woodfin Camp & Associates; Washington, Leah Washington; Wyeth, Richard Schulman/Gamma Liaison; Wyman, Steve Allen.

Glossary:
Arch, Doug Armand/Tony Stone Images; City Scape, Superstock; Minaret, Superstock; Mural, Richard Blake/Tony Stone Images; Portrait, Corbis-Bettmann; Portrait, The Granger Collection, New York; Spire, Superstock; Weaving, National Museum of the American Indian; Found Objects, Weronica Ankarorn/Harcourt Brace & Company;

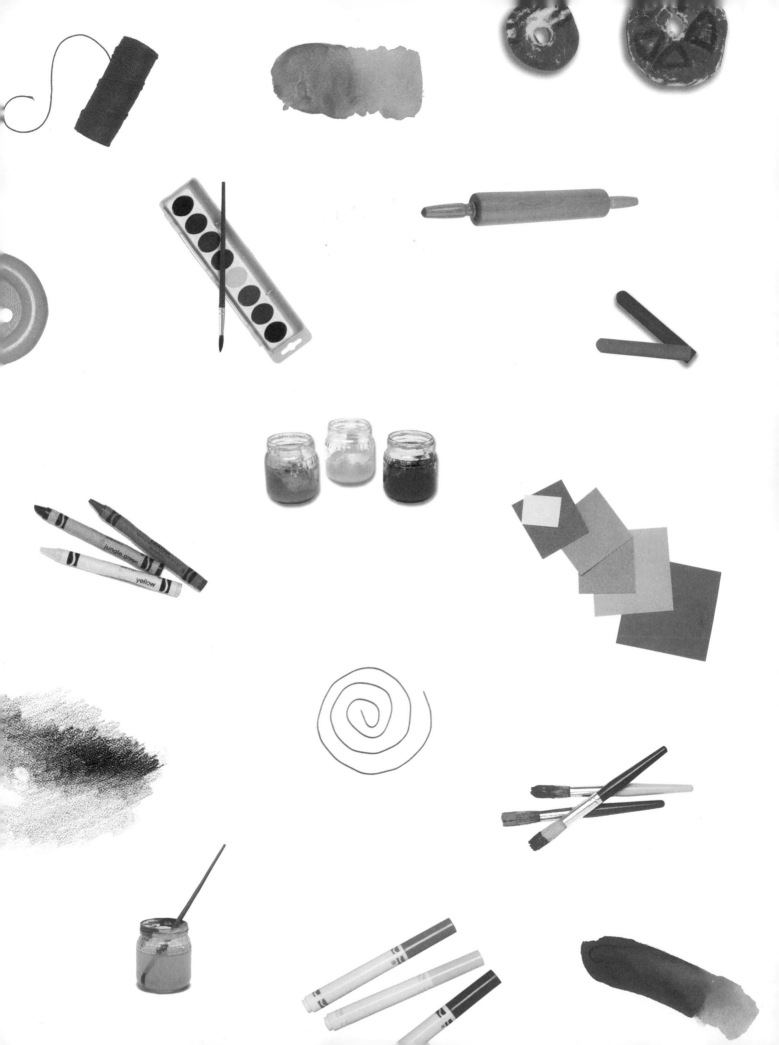